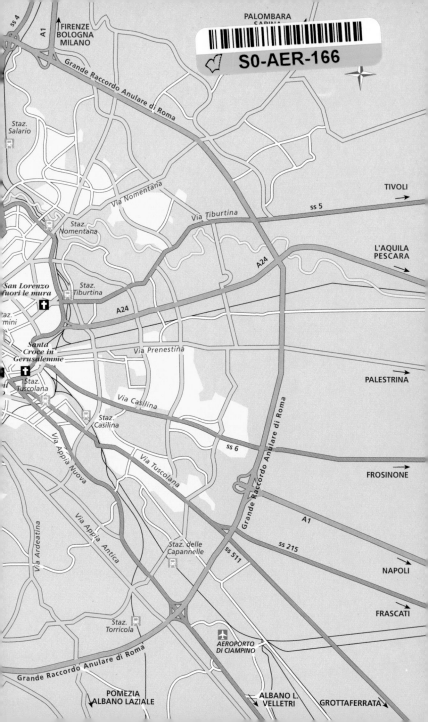

PILGRIMS
IN ROME

THE VATICAN COMMITTEE FOR THE GREAT JUBILEE OF THE YEAR 2000

PROJECT MANAGER AND EDITOR
H.E. Monsignor Francesco Gioia
Member of the Central Committee for the Great
Jubilee of the Year 2000

CONTRIBUTORS
Francesco Buranelli
The Vatican Museums
Nicolò Costa
The Basilica of St Paul
Alessandro De Angelis
The Homes of the Saints
Carmelo Dotolo
Religious Messages, Places of Worship of Other
Churches and Religious Communities
Emanuela Ghini
Spiritual Introductions
Raffaella Giuliani
The Martyrs' Sanctuaries (the Catacombs)
Historic Churches
Churches of the World's Catholics
Luca Mariani
The Basilica of St John Lateran
Historic Churches
Danilo Mazzoleni
The Basilica of St Peter, the Basilica of Santa
Maria Maggiore, the Basilica of San Lorenzo,
the Basilica of Santa Pudenziana, the Basilica
of San Clemente, Historic Churches
Mario Sensi
Rome the Eternal City, the Scala Santa and the
Sancta Sanctorum, the Basilica of Santa Croce
in Gerusalemme

MINIATURE PAINTINGS SELECTED BY
Giovanni Morello

PILGRIMS
IN ROME

THE OFFICIAL VATICAN GUIDE
FOR THE JUBILEE YEAR 2000

Pilgrims meeting the Pope outside the walls of Rome.
Detail from the Saint Ursula Cycle, by Vittore Carpaccio

CONTINUUM

CONTENTS

FOREWORD

I want to speak to you, pilgrim coming to Rome, on the occasion of the Great Jubilee of the year 2000. We believe in a mysterious God, yet we read his Word as written down in a book. We believe in an invisible God, yet we worship him under the species of bread. We believe in a God who is totally unlike us, yet we know his human name, and we know he is our Father.

Our Christian faith thrives on this two-way and yet indissoluble tension: it makes us look up to heaven, but walk on the earth. It makes us think about eternity, while binding us closely to time. It makes us dismiss material things, while spending our lives in their service.

This same duality is also present in the pilgrimage to Rome on which you are embarking. You will see a city like all others, yet unique in its mission. You will walk along the streets of a city marked by time and by man's hand, and yet the site of something that surpasses time, and goes beyond man. You will visit magnificent artistic monuments from the past, but they are still alive today, unlike the Greek temples or the Pyramids.

What, then, is this city of Rome, so profane and at the same time so mysteriously sacred? Rome is perhaps the most astonishing result of the union between our Christian faith and the physical reality of history. In Rome, almost every corner bears witness to both man's wretchedness and his capacity to be inspired by what is eternal. Why? Because Rome is the seat of the head of the Catholic Church, the Vicar of Christ, as ordered by Divine Providence.

This Mother Church of ours, without which we would not be Christians, has its very centre here in Rome. That is why the city of Rome represents to the highest degree the mysterious synthesis of heaven and earth.

Sisters and brothers, you who believe in Christ, when you arrive in this city, you will be able almost to touch with your own hand the wonderful miracle of your being a Christian, of your belonging to the Church.

Cardinal Roger Etchegaray
President of the Committee for the Jubilee Year 2000

PREFACE

A guide for the pilgrim is an indispensable tool for learning about the spiritual history and the religious messages of Rome's holy places. This guide, *Pilgrims in Rome*, produced by the Commission,* fully emphasizes the way the Christian faith is the fundamental reason for calling Rome 'The Eternal City'. Its title underlines the fact that it is intended for pilgrims, rather than ordinary tourists. It is a companion to another book intended for pilgrims, entitled *Pilgrim Prayers*. While the guide emphasizes the spiritual messages inherent in Christian monuments, the prayer book describes the celebrations that will be held in Rome's holy places. Not only are the historical and artistic aspects of each of these places described, but there is also a brief biography of the particular saint connected with it, and an account of the spiritual message that emanates from it. This is what makes this guide unique: its depiction, in a balanced and organic synthesis, of the art, the history and the spiritual meaning of each holy place, expressed in a reading based on a theme, designed to create the appropriate spiritual atmosphere before each visit, and in a message inspired by each monument.

The reader will discover all the other special features that give this work its original slant, and will certainly not fail to notice how they all fit together: the way the Eternal City has fulfilled its providential mission throughout history; the biblical themes that link the various holy places and give them their distinctive character; the churches of world Catholicism in Rome; the focus on places of worship of other Christian Churches and other religions; the unique and helpful way it points out the places in Rome where the major saints lived and died. All this is supported by modern lay-out and graphics, and by extensive illustrations, maps, plans, and itineraries.

I hope this guide will meet as fully as possible the spiritual and artistic needs of pilgrims during the Great Jubilee of the year 2000.

Archbishop Crescenzio Sepe
Secretary of the Committee for the Jubilee Year 2000

---

*The members of the Commission are: H.E. Monsignor Francesco Gioia (Chair), Ferdinando Belli (Secretary), Carlo Chenis, Antonio Collicelli, Nicolò Costa, Carmelo Dotolo, Raffaella Giuliani, Corrado Maggioni, Luca Mariani, Francesco Marinelli, Danilo Mazzoleni, Mario Sensi.

I
ROME, THE ETERNAL CITY

E TE GLORIOSA DICTA
SUNT, CIVITAS DEI (Psalm 87: 3)

*Marvellous things are said of you,
city of God*

Spiritual Introduction

*'This Church of Rome, how blessed it is!... It knows only
one God, creator of the world, and Jesus Christ, born of the
Virgin Mary, son of God the creator; and the resurrection
of the body. It unites the law and the prophets to the
Gospels and to the letters of the apostles, and its faith is
derived from there; it seals it with the water of baptism,
clothes it with the Holy Spirit, nourishes it with the
Eucharist' (Tertullian,* De praescriptione hereticorum, *36).
In the history of mankind, Rome, the heart of Christianity,
is the symbol of the providential destiny of Jerusalem, the
'Holy City' (Isaiah 52:1), 'City of Yahweh' (Isaiah 60:14),
the centre of the whole history of salvation, celebrated in
the Scriptures as the object of every human desire, the
greatest of the joys of those who love it (Psalm 137:6), the
delight of the eyes and the joy of the heart (Ezekiel 24:25).*

*The 'marvellous things' (the Hebrew term used is an
allusion to 'glory') said about Jerusalem, the goal of pilgrims
and of the children of Israel, are a manifestation of the glory of the Lord. Towards this glory peoples and nations
converge. The Church was born in Jerusalem, the city that
marks the stages in the life of Jesus Christ and where*

redemption was accomplished. She is the anticipation of the eschatological new Jerusalem (Revelation 21:1–27), the place of the total communion between God and humanity. Towards her, every man and every woman walk with their load of suffering and happiness, at a fast pace that is full of hope, or at times with the heavy tread of weariness.

The Church of Rome, expression of the whole Christian community and mother of all Churches, is projected towards the definitive city of God, place of eternal joy. In their journey towards her, all pilgrims are welcomed to a joyful pause in order to contemplate and experience awe for the beauty of being Christians. Or, in any case, to come in contact with the event of Christ who, in the Church, lives and moves towards every person 'from every nation, race, tribe and language' (Revelation 7:9). 'What do we see that the disciples did not see? The Church spread among all peoples' (St Augustine).

*The Jubilee has two centres: Rome and the Holy Land, 'in which the first Christian community appeared [... and] where God revealed himself to humanity' (*Incarnationis Mysterium, 2*). From the Holy Land, the Apostles, who were filled with the Holy Spirit on Pentecost and obedient to the words of Jesus Christ (Matthew 28:18–20), started out to spread the Gospel among Jews and pagans, throughout the whole world. From this land, 'which has marked the history of the Jewish people, and is revered by the followers of Islam' (ibid.), Peter, foundation of the Church (cf. Matthew 16:18), and Paul, Apostle of the gentiles (cf. Acts 17:21), brought the good news of salvation to Rome 'where Providence chose to place the See of the Successor of Peter', as Pope John Paul II observes in the Bull of Indiction of the Great Jubilee (ibid.).*

Historical Outline

The Capitoline she-wolf,
sacred animal and symbol of ancient Rome.

Legend has it that the basket containing the twins Romulus and Remus, the city's mythical founders, came to rest under a fig tree. The tree was still venerated in the Forum in Imperial times, showing that the early Romans followed an animistic religion. The assimilation of local and foreign deities, and the introduction into Rome of the religions of conquered cities, soon transformed the original religion into an anthropomorphic and polytheistic one. Such assimilation for political purposes was nothing new, having been known among other peoples, particularly in the Greek world. What was different, however, was that the Roman religion preserved all these influences, as was shown in the exact repetition of rituals, rules and religious forms even though, as early as the Republican era, they had already lost their original spiritual meaning.

Roma caput mundi regit orbis frena rotundi
(Rome, capital of the world, holds the reins of the round globe). This phrase dates back to the time of Emperor Diocletian, and may have been inscribed on his crown.

It was an essentially pragmatic religion, whose aim was to propitiate the gods (*pax deorum*), and to obtain favours for oneself or the community, in exchange for rituals often conducted by the beneficiary himself as priest (*pater familias*, magistrate, military commander). These ancient political, moral and religious customs were thrown into confusion, bringing about the collapse of the Republic, when Eastern religions, especially mystical and orgiastic ones, were introduced in Rome at a time of great political instability.

Julius Caesar was for a time the leading figure on the city's political scene, while the hope in the heart of every Roman citizen for the coming of a saviour (*mundi salvator*) who would restore peace was embodied in Octavianus, Caesar's great-nephew and adopted son, the future Augustus, who became the first Emperor (29 B.C.– A.D. 14).

It was during his reign that Jesus Christ was born in Bethlehem. Octavianus adopted policies that reconciled the ancient traditions of Rome's 'national' past with the need for a single leadership. He therefore accepted the title of Princeps (first among equals), and refused that of Lord, customary among Eastern rulers. The title of Augustus, bestowed on him by the Senate in

The Forum, the market place and later the city's political and administrative centre.

27 B.C., had great implications for the future. It gave him a status well above the average human being, without, however, making him a divine figure.

Augustus succeeded in his aim, and the Senate and the Roman people dedicated to him the *Ara Pacis Augustae,* a monumental altar where every year there was to be a solemn sacrifice of thanksgiving to the gods for the peace granted to the Roman world. The old religion, however, was profoundly altered by the Emperor when he proclaimed himself *Divi filius* (son of God), because Julius Caesar, his adoptive father, had been deified after his death. Augustus thus created the foundations of an Imperial cult, in which the Emperor was to be later defined as *divus* (divine) and *numen* (deity).

The deification of the Emperor is relevant to the history of the persecution of Christians, who refused to perform sacrifices to the Emperor as god, as witnessed in the Acts and Passions of the martyrs. We know about St Paul's first contact with Roman Christians through the letter he wrote to them in A.D. 56–57, in which the Apostle communicated

ROME: FROM MONARCHY TO REPUBLIC

700–600 B.C.		500–400 B.C.			300 B.C.		
	616 Etruscan supremacy	**499** Roman victory over the Latins near Lake Regillus			**367** Power shared by patricians and plebeians		**270** Reggio conquered
754–753 Rome founded		**509** Expulsion of Tarquinius Superbus		**449** Laws of the Twelve Tables		**343–341** First war against the Samnites	**272** Taranto conquered

his intention to visit them (Romans 1:10–12). Because of unexpected difficulties, Paul did not arrive in Rome until the spring of the year A.D. 61, and not as a free man, but as a prisoner. As he landed in Italy, at Pozzuoli near Naples, he was greeted by some fellow believers who were living there (Acts 28:14). Pozzuoli was one of the secondary ports where the routes from the East to Rome terminated. The presence of Christians there shows that missionary activity had followed the trade routes, both by land and by sea.

The Ara Pacis (Altar of Peace), a monument of the greatest artistic importance, dedicated to Augustus by the Senate in 9 B.C., in gratitude for the peace achieved through victorious campaigns in Spain and Gaul.

St Peter arrived in Rome soon after the date of St Paul's letter to the Romans, but nothing is known about their time together in the city. What is certain is that they were both there in A.D. 64, when a great fire, started in the vicinity of the Circus Maximus, spread through most of the city. The Emperor Nero was held responsible for it and he in turn blamed it on the Christians, and after summary trials they were put to death in the summer of A.D. 64 (Tacitus, *Annals,* 15, 44).

Peter was crucified and buried in the Vatican area, near other graves. Paul, as a Roman citizen, was beheaded near Tre Fontane, on the Via Ostiensis.

Julius Caesar was assassinated in 44 B.C. His death marked the end of the Republic.

		146 Rome occupies Greece	
240–237 Sicily and Sardinia conquered	216 Roman defeat at Cannae		129 Conquest of the East
200 B.C.		**100 B.C.**	
266–265 The Piceno region subjugated	217 Roman defeat on Lake Trasimene	202 Definitive victory over the Carthaginans	133 Spain conquered

From then on, a special decree banned the practice of Christianity, making even the use of the *nomen* (term) Christian a *crimen* (crime) (Tertullian, *Ad Nat.* 1, 3). The persecution of Christians spread throughout the Empire, lasting three hundred years, which were called 'the age of the persecutions' (there were ten, according to tradition, as a parallel to the ten plagues of Egypt), or 'the age of the martyrs'.

In A.D. 313, Emperor Constantine officially recognized Christianity, thus freeing it from its centuries-long oppression. This was the beginning of an alliance that led the Church from its status of *religio illicita* (outlawed religion) to that of Imperial Catholic Church. As the new religion received preferential treatment, the old one was increasingly driven out into the rural areas; hence the term 'paganism', meaning the religion of the *pagi* (country districts). The process of the Empire's conversion to Christianity intensified after A.D. 324. In that year Licinius Augustus, Constantine's brother-in-law and ruler of the Eastern empire, who had started to oppress Christians again, was defeated, and the absolute monarchy was restored.

The spread of Christianity. It was spread mostly through oral preaching, starting from Rome first, and then from other main centres. The motivation to convert to it sprang from the fervour of the early Christians' faith, their brotherly love, and the testimony of martyrs. Entry into the community was by a period of preparation (catechumenate), culminating in the ritual of baptism. At the heart of community life was the liturgy of the Eucharist (Justin, *1 Apology,* 65–67).

At the beginning, it was the Apostles as a group who led the Christian community, but later on local jurisdictions were formed. Indeed, during the Apostles' lifetime, there were two hierarchies: one made up of the Apostles, and the other of those whom the Apostles had put at the head of the individual communities.

The primacy of Peter, with its seat in Rome, is an institution of divine law. The office of Peter and his successors includes the role of being a sign of unity among all Churches.

The history of the Western Church is also marked by barbarian invasions, which threatened the very survival of Rome. They laid low the magnificent city (*urbs*) as a system of buildings, monuments and streets, and they would have obliterated the city (*civitas*) as a human entity, had its citizens failed to maintain their identity.

St Augustine had predicted that, as long as the Romans remained faithful to themselves, Rome would never be lost (*Sermones ad populum*). After the sack of Rome by Alaric in A.D. 410, Augustine identified in the City of God the legacy of Imperial Rome. Some years later Pope Leo the Great, who halted Attila's march on Rome in A.D. 452, in his famous speech *In natale Apostolorum*, proclaimed in prophetic words that wars had made Rome *caput mundi* (capital of the world) and that peace would make it *civitas sacerdotalis et regia* (a sacerdotal and royal city). He meant that, having been founded a second time by the Apostles Peter and Paul, the city was about to enter a new cycle in its history, one that would be truly catholic, meaning universal, with its martyrs as powerful protectors.

In the Middle Ages the fact that Rome was the place of the martyrdom of Peter and Paul was of fundamental importance, and basilicas were built over their respective tombs. During Constantine's reign, the burial places of the two Apostles and of the other martyrs became centres of worship and pilgrimage. Basilicas were built above them, or in close proximity to them, stairs and paths were built to give access to the catacombs, the most venerated crypts were decorated, and calendars were compiled recording the names of the saints.

Constantine had ordered that the basilica of St Peter be built with its high altar directly above St

The Roman Synod.
In A.D. 382 the Holy Roman Church was declared first amongst all Churches. This decision did not stem from a Council edict nor from an imperial ruling, but from the fact that it received its primacy from the words of our Lord and Saviour: *'You are Peter, and on this rock I will build my church'* (Matthew 16:18).

The Crucifixion of St Peter, *by Caravaggio (1601–1602), portrays with great drama the moment when the Apostle was crucified head down.*

Peter's tomb, as the excavations carried out between 1940 and 1949 showed. This is proof that the choice of the location of sacred monuments was not random, or dictated by the environment, but was closely related to the event commemorated there. To all intents and purposes, Roman sanctuaries are places where memory is still alive: some have remained almost untouched, while others have been turned into basilicas.

The special interest of the faithful in these places, especially the ones where the bodies of the saints were preserved, was linked to the expectation of miracles and healing being performed by the servants of Christ. Physical contact was sought in order to obtain the benefit of the healing power emanating from those holy bodies. This practice has its Gospel parallel in the episode of the woman suffering from haemorrhages: 'If I only touch his cloak, I will be made well' (Matthew 9:21 and Mark 5:28); 'She came up behind him and touched the fringe of his clothes, and immediately her bleeding stopped' (Luke 8:44).

But Rome is not only the place that brings to mind so many witnesses of the faith: it is also the seat of Peter, who was given the keys of the kingdom of heaven (Matthew 16:19), and his successors.

This sarcophagus, preserved in the Museo Nazionale Romano, in Rome, depicts the subjugation of barbarians by the Romans.

This is the reason for the pilgrimage *ad limina apostolorum* (to the doors of the Apostles) and to the *cathedra Petri* (the Chair of Peter). The practice of going on a pilgrimage *ad limina apostolorum*, which also involved a donation of money ('Peter's pence') was given a stimulus by the missionary activities of Augustine, Abbot of Sant'Andrea al Celio, and his forty fellow monks among the Anglo-Saxons who had settled in Britain.

The number of pilgrimages increased after the Germanic peoples were converted by St Boniface, the most important missionary in Germany, who had been sent there by Pope Gregory II in 719. After converting the pagans, Boniface devoted himself to purifying and strengthening Christian life. He was convinced that the necessary condition for the growth of a local Church was the maintenance of close links with Rome. Therefore, in 743, he made all the Bishops gathered together for the first Council of the Eastern Franks pronounce an oath of allegiance to the Pope. The alliance of the Popes with the Franks (the Holy Roman Empire) and the split with Byzantium completed the task: Rome was reinstated as the capital of the world.

From the ninth century onwards, a new system of penance was established, whereby the appropriate penance for many sins committed over a period of time included a pilgrimage of atonement before full absolution could be obtained. Rome became the favourite destination of these penitential pilgrimages, and monasteries and hospitals were built along the routes for the welfare of pilgrims and the sick.

Pilgrimages to Rome increased considerably during the Jubilee of the year 1300, proclaimed by Pope Boniface VIII, reflecting a spontaneous and genuine popular spiritual impulse at a time when it was impossible to reach the Holy Land.

The **cathedra Petri** *(Chair of Peter), preserved in St Peter's, is an oak chair decorated with strips of ivory and twelve panels depicting the labours of Hercules and six fabulous beasts. The ivory panels showing the stories of Hercules probably date back to the time of Emperor Charles the Bald (875–877). Carved in classical style, they were set into the Emperor's throne, which was later donated to the Pope by the Emperor himself.*

Fragment of a fresco *by Giotto, depicting Pope Boniface VIII proclaiming the first Jubilee in 1300 (St John Lateran).*

Because of political events, the Jubilees of 1800 (Pius VI and Pius VII) and 1850 (Pius IX) were not celebrated; the 1875 Jubilee was celebrated without ceremony.

Extraordinary Jubilees
The first one was declared by Leo X in 1518, to help Poland in its war against the Turks.
The number of these is uncertain: the 1,900th and 1,950th anniversaries of the Redemption in 1933 (Pius XI) and 1983 (John Paul II) are well known.

After deliberation, Pope Boniface VIII decided that the Jubilee should be celebrated only once every 100 years; Pope Benedict XII reduced the time to 50 years, until Pope Paul II (1464–1471) established that celebrations should take place every 25 years.

Initially the tombs and relics of the Apostles Peter and Paul were the only two reference points for Jubilee pilgrimages. Later, in 1350, Pope Urban VI added the basilica of St John Lateran, which is the cathedral of Rome, and in 1390, on the occasion of the Holy Year, Pope Boniface IX extended the duty to include Santa Maria Maggiore, the first sanctuary dedicated to the Virgin Mary in Western Christendom.

These became the 'patriarchal basilicas' where, from the 1500 Jubilee onwards, simultaneous ceremonies were conducted by proxies while the Pope officiated in St Peter's.

Later on, in the last quarter of the sixteenth century, the practice, initiated by St Philip Neri, took root of visiting the seven basilicas: St Peter's, St Paul's, Santa Maria Maggiore, St John Lateran, Santa Croce in Gerusalemme, San Lorenzo and San Sebastiano.

Romans had to extend their visit to the four major basilicas for thirty days, whether consecutive or not, while for people from outside Rome this duty was reduced to fifteen days, consecutive or not. In 1900, Pope Leo XIII reduced this duty to twenty and ten days respectively. Eventually, in the 1933 Jubilee, Pope Pius XI reduced the visits to three, for both Roman and non-Roman visitors, with the possibility of completing them in the same day.

On the occasion of the Holy Year of 1950, Pope Pius XII prescribed one visit only for each basilica, with no time requirement.

On the last pier is the bronze statue of St Peter, seated on a nineteenth-century marble throne, giving a blessing and with the keys in his left hand. Recent research has confirmed that it was most likely made by Arnolfo di Cambio in the late thirteenth century. Other scholars, on the other hand, maintain that it is an early Christian sculpture, dating back to the fifth century, and moved into the basilica in the Middle Ages.

The right foot of the statue shows obvious evidence of wear, from the tradition, existing since the Middle Ages, of pilgrims kissing it. Above it on the pier is a roundel dedicated to Pius IX, who was Pope for the longest time (32 years, from 1846 to 1878), longer even than Peter. Along the frieze of the entablature runs a wall inscription on a gold background, recording in Greek and in Latin the words used by Jesus to found the Church.

The focal point of the basilica is Bernini's bronze canopy. The four large statues, five metres high, inside the niches at the foot of the piers supporting the dome were commissioned by Pope Urban VIII (1643), the one of St Longinus being by Bernini himself. Under the canopy, Maderno's Confessio is permanently lit by 99 lamps, burning on the site of Peter's tomb. The first chapel along the right aisle is named after the *Pietà*, the famous marble group by Michelangelo which is housed there. It was commissioned by the Cardinal Legate of Charles VIII to Pope Alexander VI, and is the only work signed by the master (his signature is visible on the sash across Mary's chest). Because of damage suffered in 1971, it is now protected by a thick sheet of glass.

On the right, under the memorial to Leo XII, is the entrance to the Chapel of the Relics, containing a valuable

In the nave, near the main entrance, there is a round porphyry slab. It was on this that Charlemagne knelt to be crowned Emperor by Pope Leo III on Christmas night, A.D. 800. This ritual was repeated by 21 successive monarchs. In the illustration: the coronation of Charlemagne, taken from Grandes Chroniques de France, *a French manuscript of the fourteenth century.*

The canopy, with its spiral columns 20 metres high, was built by Bernini on the orders of Urban VIII in 1624.

wooden crucifix attributed to Pietro Cavallini. In the next chapel, dedicated to St Sebastian, there are memorials to Pius XI and Pius XII, who were Popes during the twentieth century, as well as the tomb of Innocent XI. The third chapel, named after the Blessed Sacrament, has a gate designed by Francesco Borromini, and a gilt bronze tabernacle by Bernini (1674) in front of the Trinity altarpiece, a seventeenth-century work by Pietro da Cortona. Noteworthy in the Gregorian Chapel, by Giacomo della Porta (1583), is the venerated image of the Madonna of Succour, dating back to the eleventh century, and already in the earlier basilica.

The right transept contains the monument to Pope Clement XIII, shown kneeling in prayer, one of the masterpieces of Antonio Canova (1784–1792). The bronze Chair of St Peter takes centre stage in the middle of the apse. It was made by Bernini (1656–1665), and it incorporates the chair, made of wood with ivory panels, that belonged to Charles the Bald in the ninth century, and later became a possession of the Popes. Known as *Cathedra Petri*, its panels depict mythological scenes from the labours of Hercules, and a king, who could be either Charles the Bald or Charlemagne. On Christmas night in the year 800, Charlemagne was crowned Emperor in St Peter's by Pope Leo III.

The chair is supported by the large statues of the four great Doctors of the Church, and above it the dove of the Holy Spirit appears in the centre of an alabaster window, in a setting of praising angels and putti. To the right of the raised area of the apse there is a niche containing the monument to Urban VIII by Bernini (1627–1647), while to the left is the monument to Paul III, sculpted by Guglielmo della Porta (1551–1575).

The Chapel of the Column contains a marble altarpiece by Alessandro Algardi, depicting

The memorial monument to Clement XIII
was executed by Antonio Canova between 1784 and 1792.

the meeting of St Leo the Great with Attila (1646–1650), and a much venerated image of the Virgin Mary.

Beyond the left transept, and separate from the basilica, we find the Sacristy, where, on the right, are listed the names of all the Popes buried in St Peter's, from the Apostle himself to John Paul I. The mortal remains of St Gregory the Great, initiator of important works in the earlier basilica, and a great Doctor of the Church, are preserved in the Clementine Chapel, which also contains the tomb of Pius VII, by the Danish neo-classical sculptor Bertel Thorvaldsen (1823).

In the left nave is the Chapel of the Choir, designed by Maderno. Next comes the Chapel of the Presentation, containing the monument to John XXIII by Emilio Greco. Beyond this is the baptistery, whose font is a porphyry sarcophagus dating back to the time of Hadrian, and later used as a tomb for the Emperor Otto II.

The Vatican Grottos occupy the area beneath the central nave, and include part of the Vatican cemetery. There are several mausoleums, some with clear evidence of Christian conversion, and fragments of sculptures, walls and architectural elements belonging to the earliest place of worship. The Grottos also contain the tombs of many Popes, from St Peter to John Paul I. Various chapels open onto the visitor's route. Among these, the one closest to Peter's tomb is the Clementine Chapel, or Chapel of St Peter. Commissioned by Clement VIII, it is richly decorated in stucco and multicoloured marble. The altar was built in place of an earlier one, of the sixth century. In the area

The Chapel of St Peter, in the Vatican Grottos, was decorated under Clement VIII.

The Pietà, by Michelangelo, carved from a single block of Carrara marble in 1499, can be seen in the former Chapel of St Petronilla, the first in the basilica's right-hand nave.

of the Confessio is the niche of the Pallii, important because inside it can be recognized traces of Peter's tomb as it was in the second century, when a small memorial shrine was built above it.

The most important excavations were carried out between 1940 and 1957, and clarified the complex topography of the area, and the various archaeological periods involved. Of great interest are the mausoleums from the Imperial Roman era, usually with decoration in stucco, mosaic or frescoes. In some there is clear evidence of Christian iconography. One is the mausoleum of the Julii, containing fragments of a third-century wall mosaic with pictures of Christ the Sun, the Good Shepherd, the prophet Jonah and a fisherman.

THE LARGEST CHURCHES IN THE WORLD
(These lengths are engraved on the floor of the central nave of St Peter's)

(1) St Peter's in the Vatican: 186.36 m

(2) St Paul's, London: 158.10 m

(3) The Duomo in Florence: 149.28 m

(4) Sacred Heart of Jesus, Brussels: 140.94 m

(5) Immaculate Conception, Washington D.C.: 139.14 m

(6) Rheims Cathedral (France): 138.69 m

(7) The Duomo in Milan and Cologne Cathedral: 134.94 m

(8) Speyer Cathedral (Germany) 134 m

(9) San Petronio, Bologna: 132.54 m

(10) Seville Cathedral: 132 m

(11) St Paul's outside the Walls, Rome: 131.66 m

(12) Notre Dame, Paris: 130 m

(13) St Vitus, Prague: 124 m

(14) Toledo Cathedral: 122 m

(15) St John Lateran, Rome: 121.84 m

(16) La Plata Cathedral (Argentina): 120 m

(17) Mexico City Cathedral: 119.55 m

(18) Antwerp Cathedral (Belgium): 118.60 m

(19) Santa Giustina, Padua: 118.50 m

(20) Esztergom Catherdral (Hungary), and Ferrara Cathedral: 118 m

(21) Basilica of Santa Maria degli Angeli, Assisi: 114.76 m

(22) St Paul's, Brasilia: 111.45 m

(23) Westminster Cathedral, London: 110 m

(24) Hagia Sophia, Istanbul: 109.57 m

(25) Cathedral of the Holy Cross, Boston: 103.50 m

(26) Basilica of the Virgin Mary, Gdansk (Poland): 103.50 m

(27) St Patrick's Cathedral, New York: 101.19 m

1725 also saw the building of the Chapel of the Crucifix, known today as the Chapel of the Blessed Sacrament, to house the miraculous fourteenth-century wooden crucifix.

Many of these layers of history and centuries-old artistic and architectural treasures, gathered under one roof, went up in smoke during that terrible night in 1823; an integrated expression of art, architecture and religion was almost entirely lost.

Popes, architects and Catholic intellectuals were called upon to meet the challenge of reproducing its lost authenticity: a particularly difficult challenge at a time which, following the age of Enlightenment, was dominated by profane and sacrilegious ideas.

Figures from the field of culture, literature and politics urged Leo XII to start rebuilding the basilica. So, on 25 January 1825, the Pope sent all the bishops the letter *Ad plurimas easque gravissimas,* asking them to start collecting donations from the faithful, in order to set in motion what was to be the largest church building project in the whole of the nineteenth century. Believers from all over the world responded to the appeal; while many sent money, the Viceroy of Egypt donated alabaster columns, and Tsar Nicholas I sent blocks of malachite, which were used for the two side altars in the transept.

Work started in September 1826, with Belli as architect, following Valadier's preliminary plan: the Arch of Galla Placidia was demolished and the four-sided portico was reinstated.

On 5 October 1840, Pope Gregory XVI solemnly consecrated the altar of the Confessio, with its restored canopy above.

The wooden crucifix, dating from the fourteenth century, and attributed to Tino di Camaino. Tradition has it that, in 1370, Christ inclined his head towards St Bridget, deep in prayer at his feet.

On the inside, the basilica is 131.66 metres long, 65 metres wide and 29.70 metres high. It has 80 monolithic columns made of granite from Montórfano, which divide it into five naves, the central one of which is 24.60 metres wide.

The four-sided portico, built by Guglielmo Calderini in 1928, is 70 metres long. On the front there are 10 monolithic columns, 10 metres high, made of pink granite from Baveno; on each side there is a double row of columns, and on the side facing the Tiber a triple row, 146 in all.

High up inside there are 36 frescoes depicting events in the saint's life with, underneath, a frieze containing the portraits of all 265 Popes, from Peter to John Paul II.

Art and Architecture

PRACTICAL INFORMATION
Via Ostiense 186.
📞 06 541 03 41.
🚌 23, 170, 223.
Ⓜ B San Paolo.
Opening hours
7.30 a.m.–7 p.m. (6 p.m.
September–March) (last
admissions: 15 minutes
before closing time).

On entering from the west through a wrought-iron gate, one is immediately struck by the solemn and majestic statue of St Paul, carved in Carrara marble by Giuseppe Obici (1817–1878), and by the vast four-sided portico in front of the façade, built by Guglielmo Calderini between 1890 and 1928 to the original design by Luigi Poletti. An *atrium* enclosed by a portico existed in front of the basilica in ancient times, but Calderini's building, partly because it

The mosaic of the triumphal arch

The bell-tower
of St Paul's as it is now. The original, dating from the fourteenth century, like the eighteenth-century portico, survived the 1823 fire, but was destroyed during reconstruction work.

The Gregorian porch

The library
contains the Bible of Charles the Bald, the oldest existing Carolingian manuscript.

The Arch of Galla Placidia: a mistaken interpretation of the two verses written on its edge has led to the belief that the arch was commissioned by the Emperor Honorius, brother of Galla Placidia.

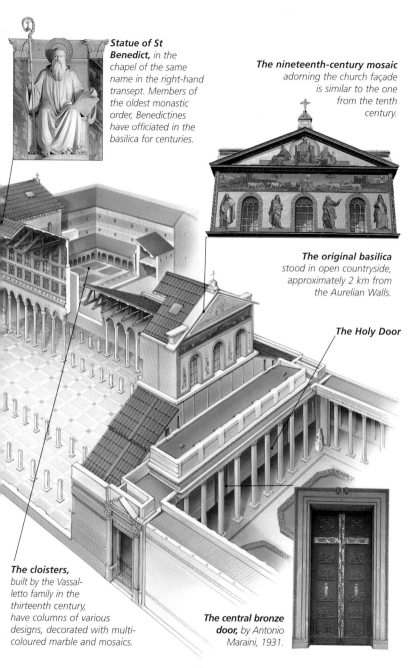

Statue of St Benedict, in the chapel of the same name in the right-hand transept. Members of the oldest monastic order, Benedictines have officiated in the basilica for centuries.

The nineteenth-century mosaic adorning the church façade is similar to the one from the tenth century.

The original basilica stood in open countryside, approximately 2 km from the Aurelian Walls.

The Holy Door

The cloisters, built by the Vassalletto family in the thirteenth century, have columns of various designs, decorated with multi-coloured marble and mosaics.

The central bronze door, by Antonio Maraini, 1931.

is so much larger, bears no resemblance to it.

The idea of the four sides, each 70 metres long, came from the belief that they were essential to the reconstruction of a true early Christian basilica. Both the north and south sides have solid walls covered in travertine marble; the principal frontage has three rows of imposing columns, the north and south sides have two, and the narthex one. The side walls are decorated with medallions representing the symbols of the Evangelists, portraits of St Paul's disciples, and symbols of early Christian worship.

The upper part of the façade is decorated with mosaics based on designs by Filippo Agricola (1795–1857) and Nicola Consoni (1814–1884), and completed between 1854 and 1874. The lower section, between the windows, shows the prophets of the Old Testament: Isaiah, Jeremiah, Ezekiel and Daniel. The middle section shows the Lamb of God on the mountain of Paradise, with four rivers, symbolizing the Gospels, flowing from it, and twelve lambs (the Apostles) drinking from them. They appear separate from Jerusalem and Bethlehem, the holy cities that here provide only the geographical and

onize Rome's still large pagan population. However, another suggestion is that the *domus ecclesia* was built directly on top of the ruins of the house of the Laterani; under it have been found what are thought to have been the remains of a building dating from the Severan period (192–235), later used as barracks for the Emperor's personal guard, the *equites singulares*. Constantine had the barracks demolished after dissolving the guard, which was loyal to Maxentius, whom he had defeated at the battle of the Milvian Bridge in 312, and built the early Christian basilica. It was first dedicated to the Saviour, and later, during the papacy of Gregory I (590–604), also to Sts John the Baptist and John the Evangelist. Pope Lucius II gave it its present name in 1144.

The early building was very similar in plan to the present one, with five naves, separated by magnificent marble columns. The transept was limited to

Historical events.

The most important events associated with the basilica include the five Ecumenical Councils of 1123, 1139, 1179, 1215 and 1512. There in 1133 Pope Innocent II crowned King Lothair III of Germany as Emperor Lothair II. In 1223, Charles of Anjou was crowned King of Sicily, and in 1312 Henry VII of Luxemburg was created Emperor. In 1347 the newly knighted tribune and reformer Cola di Rienzo proclaimed the Lex Regia. Pope Eugenius IV put the basilica under the care of secular clergy, who ran it from 1450. The Chapter, which takes precedence over that of St Peter's in all the great church ceremonies, consists of a Cardinal archpriest and 22 canons.

The legend of Constantine's leprosy is associated with the founding of the basilica. Sts Peter and Paul appeared to him in a dream, telling him he would be cured if he was baptized. He sent for Pope Sylvester I (314–335), who baptized him and cured his leprosy; he then had the church built as a sign of his gratitude.

the three central naves; the two on either side, which are shorter, ended in two square chambers that extended beyond the side walls.

The basilica was richly decorated in gold and marble, and was called 'golden'; papal archives record Constantine's lavish donations of these materials. Legend also has it that in it were preserved the Ark of the Covenant, the Tablets of the Law, the Golden Candelabrum, the Tabernacle and Aaron's priestly robes.

The high altar was placed in the crossing, with the papal throne directly in line with it. The widest and highest of the central naves rested on 30 columns of yellow Numidian marble, probably of the same length as those under the eighteenth-century organ.

The arches were decorated with panels of the same marble, and there were mosaics with a gold background. The dominant colour was yellow, and this may be why it was called 'golden'. The side naves were supported inside the perimeter wall on 40 columns in green Peloponnesian marble, which were shorter and needed large plinths to bring them up to the slope of the ceiling, with an arch supporting a wall that was pierced to let light through.

Mosaic pavements, *below the central nave, found during excavations in 1934.*

CHRONOLOGY

300		400	800–900
313 *Constantine gives the land belonging to the Laterani to Pope Melchiades*	**455** *The church ransacked by Vandals under Genseric*	**896** *The church damaged by an earthquake*	
314–318 *The church of five naves built*			
324 *The basilica consecrated by Pope Sylvester I and dedicated to the Saviour*	**c. 457** *The church restored by Pope Leo the Great*	**904–911** *The church rebuilt under Pope Sergius III*	
	Pope Leo the Great		

The basilica suffered many disasters over the course of the centuries, and as many operations to repair and alter it.

In 455, Vandals under Genseric ransacked the church and stole the priceless treasures it contained. It was restored by Pope Leo the Great (440–461). Some centuries later, in 896, it suffered considerable damage in an earthquake, and Pope Sergius III (904–911) commissioned extensive works to reinforce it, and also had the gallery decorated with mosaics.

Further restoration and embellishment was carried out in the twelfth century under Alexander III (1159–1181), who had the now lost east façade built, and Clement III (1187–1191), who decorated it with mosaics, also lost. Nicholas IV (1288–1292) added further sumptuous decoration, including the large mosaic in the apse, executed by Jacopo Torriti and Jacopo da Camerino.

The apse of St John had a choir ambulatory, that is, a semicircular processional path in the style of the early Christian cemetery basilicas, the only example of this rare

The primitive basilica, in severe style, was dedicated to Christ the Saviour, because an image, described in Greek as 'acheiropoieta', or 'not made by human hand', is traditionally said to have miraculously appeared during the consecration of the church built by order of Pope Sylvester I in 324. The image was then reproduced in mosaic on the façade, and was considered miraculous throughout the Middle Ages.

One of the fifteen statues on the façade of St John Lateran.

4	1300 The first Holy Year declared		1586 Domenico Fontana executes the north façade		1732 A competition to build the main façade is announced	c. 1878 Pope Leo XIII has the apse rebuilt
rch icated *John*	**1308** *The church destroyed in a fire*	**1377** *The Popes return from Avignon*				
00	*1300*	*1500*	*1600*		*1700*	*1800*
		1361 *The church burned down for the second time*	**1562–1567** *Pirro Ligorio plans the wooden ceiling*	**1646** *Borromini rebuilds the interior*	**1732–1740** *Alessandro Galilei executes the façade*	
	1309 *The papacy transferred to Avignon*					*Pope Leo XIII*

St Leo the Great *restored the basilica after its sacking by the Vandals in 455.*

Pope Gregory XI (1370–1378), *in a fresco by Giorgio Vasari.*

feature in early medieval Rome. The existing twelfth-century throne, by Nicola d'Angelo, a Roman worker in marble, was placed in the primitive apse.

In 1308 the basilica was partially destroyed in a fire and immediately rebuilt by Clement V (1305–1314). After another fire in 1361, restoration work was carried out under Popes Urban V (1362–1370), who was responsible for the canopy over the papal altar, and Gregory XI (1370–1378). Pope Martin V (1417–1431) had the celebrated marble masons of the Cosmati school make the polychromatic pavement, and Pope Eugenius IV (1431–1447) commissioned various renovations from the architect Filarete. Under Innocent VIII (1484–1492) the arch in front of the papal altar was built, and under Pius IV (1559–1565), the east façade and the ceiling, later gilded by order of Pius V (1566–1572).

The front of the basilica had three windows with pointed arches, bearing an image of the Redeemer, and was preceded by a portico with six columns. The Patriarchate adjoined the basilica; the Pope's seat was, in fact, the Lateran basilica, and under the influence of Constantinople it was changed from a bishopric (*episcopium*) into a patriarchate (*patriarchium*).

The Pope was attended by seminarians chosen from among the pupils of the *orphanotrophium* (orphanage) or *schola cantorum* (choir school), the former at St John's and the latter at St Peter's, or by lay people from the city's noble families who took seats in the *cubiculari*, or raised pews.

So for about a thousand years, from its foundation until the beginning of the fourteenth century, the basilica of St John Lateran and the buildings that sprang up around it were the seat of the papacy. In addition, when it became the cathedral of Rome, it took precedence over the basilicas of St Peter and St Paul, made sacred by their apostolic relics. But when it was decided to move the papal residence to Avignon, in France, from 1304 to 1377, St John was abandoned, and on their return to Rome, the Popes chose to settle first in Santa Maria in Trastevere and then finally in the Vatican.

Seeing the dreadful state the church was in, Sixtus V (1585–1590) decided to undertake major restoration works. He commissioned his trusted architect, Domenico Fontana, to build the Lateran Palace as a papal summer residence, in what was then open country.

Later, however, the Quirinal hill seemed a more suitable location, perhaps because of its strategic position. This meant that the Lateran Palace lost all its magnificence, and was left abandoned until the middle of the seventeenth century.

Borromini's restoration.
Innocent X put Francesco Borromini in charge of restoring the basilica four years before the Jubilee of 1650, and the work was completed in 1649. The most elegant of the three designs was selected and five large arches were opened, separated by pairs of huge pilasters, between which were 12 niches, later filled by statues of the apostles. On the sides of the upper part of the nave, rectangular windows above the arcades alternate with paintings set inside oval frames. The wooden ceiling was retained, although the architect had intended to build a barrel vault.

Interior of St John Lateran.

Art and Architecture

PRACTICAL INFORMATION
4 Piazza San Giovanni
in Laterano.
C 06 77 20 79 91.
🚌 4, 16, 81, 85, 87, 714
and other routes serving
Piazza San Giovanni.
Ⓜ A San Giovanni. 🚋 30b.
**Opening hours: Church
and cloisters** 7 a.m.–7 p.m.
(6 p.m. Mon–Fri,
October–March).
Museum 9 a.m.–1 p.m.,
3–5 p.m. Mon–Fri.
(currently closed for
restoration).
Entry charge for cloisters
and museum. 🚻 📷 🚪

In 1732 Pope Clement XII (Corsini) (1730–1740) announced a competition to build a new façade for the basilica. The contest led to heated controversy, but it was important because it demonstrated the different styles of eighteenth-century church architects. The winner was Alessandro Galilei, from Florence, who started work in the same year. Instead of following Baroque conventions, he went back to the monumental style of the late Renaissance. His imposing façade, preceded by a short flight of stairs, has a single order of pilaster strips and engaged columns, divided laterally into three sections, the one in the centre standing proud of the rest, and five bays.

The tall pilaster strips and the two pairs of columns supporting the triangular pediment rest on a tall stylobate, or base, and have Corinthian capitals. Above the portico, with its architrave and five openings, is a loggia, also consisting of five arches, of which the central one is a large Palladian window. The entablature, with a balustrade running the entire length of the façade, carries fifteen colossal statues. In the centre stands the Redeemer, between St John the Baptist and St John the Evangelist; they are flanked by the twelve Doctors of the Greek and Latin Churches, representing the doctrinal unity of the Church of Christ. Galilei had no interest in *chiaroscuro* or the other pictorial values the various elements offered, but set himself the problem of perspective as a

**Reliquary
of Clement XII
(1730–1740),**
*in the museum of
St John Lateran.*

The baptistery, often restored, is from the era of Constantine. Its present octagonal form, from the fifth century, was a model for baptisteries throughout the Christian world.

The Pope alone may celebrate Mass at the papal altar. Its Gothic canopy, with frescoes, dates from the fourteenth century.

The side door is opened once every 25 years, for Holy Year.

Length: at 130 metres, the basilica is 1.5 m longer than Constantine's original basilica of St Peter's. The central nave is 16 metres wide and 87 long.

The Egyptian obelisk is the tallest (at 47 metres including the base), and the most ancient in Rome, which has 13 obelisks, more than any other city in the world.

Statues of Christ, the two St Johns and the Doctors of the Church.

The Corsini Chapel, built in 1734 by A. Galilei, above an ancient cemetery.

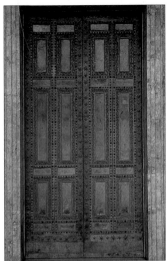

The great bronze doors
at the basilica's central entrance.

measure of elegance and taste. In fact, the proportional relationship between the first and second levels is entirely new, since the lower part is extended lengthwise while the upper has the usual dimensions.

This novel solution was necessary because the new façade looked down a long, straight street, the Strada Giulia, making it difficult to view it from the front. The architect therefore extended his design sideways, greatly enlarging the lower part and using the steps up to the entrance to increase the effect.

The bottom level of the portico, reached by one of the great wrought iron gates, has a low barrel vault with stucco coffers, and in the centre the arms of Clement XII. The five doors correspond to the five naves, and the central door has priceless authentic bronze panels, taken from the ancient Curia in the Forum. A curious belief is associated with them; expectant mothers touch them, in the hope that they will give birth to a boy.

The last door on the right, defined as the Holy Door, is opened only once every 25 years, for the Jubilee, by demolishing the wall behind it. The ritual was performed for the first time in this basilica by Martin V in 1423 and later extended to the other Roman basilicas.

The basilica is 130 metres long and has five naves, with a wide transept and a huge apse, completely rebuilt during the pontificate of Leo XIII (1878–1903). Its architecture and decoration go back to Borromini and its many statues and paintings clearly express his key idea: the Church, whose cornerstone is Christ, is built on the foundation of the Apostles and the prophets. The wooden ceiling is original, dating from the sixteenth century; it was probably designed by Pirro Ligorio between 1562 and 1567 and is decorated with the arms of Pius IV (dei Medici), during whose papacy the work was carried out. Nearer the front wall are the arms of Pius VI (Braschi) (1775–1799), who had the ceiling repaired.

In the central nave, in niches set in the pilasters, are statues of the Apostles, made in the early 1700s. Above the niches, note the high reliefs in stucco of *Scenes from the Old and New Testaments,* executed in the sixteenth century by Alessandro Algardi and his collaborators, who created a 'biblical concordance', that is to say, the life of Jesus the Messiah, as prefigured in the Old Testament. Higher up, in oval stucco frames, are portraits of the prophets, painted in the late 1600s or early 1700s.

A number of chapels open off the outermost side aisles. The second on the right is the nineteenth-century Torlonia Chapel, in the form of

The competition held in 1732 to build the present façade was won by Alessandro Galilei. 23 architects, who submitted 27 original wooden models of their finished design, took part.

The precious reliquary above the altar of the Sacrament contains a fragment of the table at which Jesus and the Apostles are said to have eaten the Last Supper. The relic is exhibited on Easter Sunday.

The façade of the Lateran basilica with the statues of Christ the Redeemer, St John the Baptist, St John the Evangelist and the eight Doctors of the Latin and Greek Church.

The Torlonia Chapel, *designed in the late neo-classical style by A. Raimondi (1830–1850), is dedicated to St John Nepomucene.*

a Greek cross with a dome, one of the latest chapels of the Roman aristocracy. The third on the right, the Massimo Chapel, was built by Giacomo Della Porta in 1590; it has a crucifix by Sermoneta (1575) on the altar. The first on the left, the Corsini Chapel, was built by Alessandro Galilei between 1732 and 1735. The tomb of Clement XII, however, is the work of Giovan Battista Maini. The third chapel on the left, from the early 1600s, is by Onorio Longhi, and the fourth was built by Giovanni Antonio De Rossi in 1675.

The transept was completely rebuilt to a design by Giacomo Della Porta during the papacy of Clement VIII (1592–1605). Its important frescoes were painted by well-known late sixteenth-century Mannerist artists under the direction of the Cavalier d'Arpino.

High up at the far end of the right arm of the transept is the organ, dating from 1598. Opposite, in the left arm, is the richly decorated altar of the Sacrament, made to the design of Pier Paolo Olivieri in 1600. The Colonna Chapel, built by Girolamo Rainaldi in 1625, also opens off the transept and has beautiful wooden stalls ornamented with statues of saints. To the right of the chapel, under the twentieth-century monument to Leo XIII, is the entrance to the sacristy. In it is an *Annunciation*, painted by Marcello Venusti in 1555 after a design by Michelangelo, and on the altar a late sixteenth-century *Magdalene*, attributed to Scipione Pulzone.

In the centre of the transept is the Gothic canopy, made during the papacy of Urban V (the Frenchman Guillaume de Grimoard), using funds provided by Charles V of France. It is the work of Giovanni di Stefano; the twelve panels, painted by Barna da Siena in 1367–1368, were restored and retouched

Papal throne, *exhibited in the cloisters. It has a seat dating from classical antiquity, and spiral columns, and is the oldest papal throne in existence.*

about a century later by Antoniazzo Romano and Fiorenzo di Lorenzo.

Up above, behind a metal grille, are a set of nineteenth-century reliquaries (replacing the fourteenth-century originals), which contain relics of the heads of St Peter and St Paul. Under the canopy is the papal altar, at which the Pope alone is allowed to celebrate Mass. It is modern, but encloses the ancient wooden altar used until the fourth century by the first thirteen Popes, from St Peter to St Sylvester. The tomb of Martin V (Colonna), under the altar, by Simone Ghini (1443), is worth noting.

Borromini's greatest achievement was his remodelling of the tombs of the Popes and Cardinals which were in the old basilica. Innocent X had ordered that once the work of reconstruction was completed, the tombs, or parts of them, were to be rebuilt inside the restored church; the tombs were therefore dismantled and moved to the cloisters when reconstruction started.

When Cardinal Fabio Chigi was elected Pope in 1655, as Alexander VII, Borromini was able to act more freely. He kept a fragment of each tomb and inserted it into the new monument he had designed, using the medieval fragments like relics to be preserved in their new setting, in perfect harmony with the style he was imposing on the renovated church. And since there were oval windows in the outside walls of the side naves, and the funerary monuments could not be placed against them, Borromini incorporated them into the new tombs, so that they appeared to be elements of the design itself. He took great pains to vary motifs and aesthetic solutions, in order to give

The statue of St Andrew, with those of Sts Peter, John, James, Bartholomew and Simon, is in the left aisle.

The cloisters, reached through a door at the far end of the left aisle, are a masterpiece of Cosmatesque art. Small arches rest on pairs of small columns, of different forms and with different capitals. The cloisters, on a square plan, were built between 1225 and 1236 by members of the Vassalletto family. In the centre of the cloister is a ninth-century well-head. The vaults of the ambulatories rest on columns with Ionic capitals, of a later date. The four porticos contain many fragments of the ancient basilica. The most beautiful of these are the remains of the episcopal throne of Nicholas IV (1288–1292), once in the apse, a fifth-century stone head of a woman, believed by some to be a portrait of St Helena, and the thirteenth-century tomb of Cardinal Annibaldi della Molara, attributed to Arnolfo di Cambio, other parts of which are now in the church itself.

the faithful real evidence of the centuries-old religious life of the Lateran basilica, as if presenting an ideal collection of mementos from the past.

A fragment of a fresco by Giotto has been incorporated into the monument of Boniface VIII; it shows the Pope proclaiming the first Holy Year (1300). It can be dated to the period immediately before the Assisi frescoes, which, as we recall, include the *Dream of Innocent III*, showing the ancient basilica with a typical Romanesque bell-tower. In the centre of the tomb of Sergius IV, who died in 1012, we note a bas-relief of the Pope giving a blessing, inserted into a frame by Borromini formed of the stars that appear on the coat of arms of Alexander VII (Chigi).

Leaving the basilica by the door at the far end of the right arm of the transept, we note the external façade of 1589, by Domenico Fontana, superimposed on the old façade, of which the surviving entablature and the two side bell-towers can be seen. The upper of its two orders of five arches, called the Loggia of Benedictions, has frescoes by a group of Mannerist painters working under the direction of Cesare Nebbia and Giovanni Guerra. The loggia is joined to the Lateran Palace, just as the Pulpit of Boniface was to the Patriarchate. In the same way, the façade, with the identical motif of blind arches aligned with the architectural order of the ground level, is connected to the rest of the Palatine chapel of the Patriarchate (the Scala Santa). Passing the left wall of a nineteenth-century construction built by Leo XIII, the visitor reaches the fourth-century baptistery, the earliest of its kind and the only known example in Rome.

Sixtus III (432–440) had it completely rebuilt on an octagonal plan, using eight

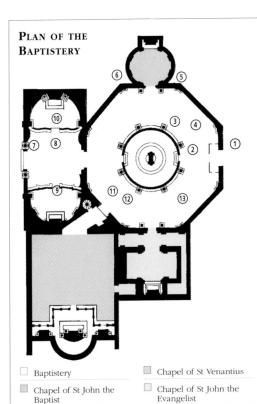

PLAN OF THE BAPTISTERY

☐ Baptistery

☐ Chapel of St Venantius

☐ Chapel of St John the Baptist

☐ Chapel of St John the Evangelist

porphyry columns that had been cut but not used, and adding an atrium. Pope Hilarius (461–468) built three chapels, two of which survive, though with radical alterations. The one farthest to the left, with the original bronze doors made by Umberto da Piacenza in 1196, is dedicated to St John the Evangelist. Its original mosaic of birds and flowers still adorns the vault. The second chapel, on the opposite side, retains its door panels, taken from the Baths of Caracalla; silver was used in their casting, and they 'sing' when opened. The chapel is dedicated to St John the Baptist and was built by

The Lateran baptistery
is in the form of an octagonal structure, with brick walls. Its glazed windows bear the arms of Pius XI, who was responsible for the excavations of 1925. The outlines of windows blocked up when various restoration works were carried out can be seen in the walls. The dome has eight oval windows.

The font *was arranged so that water entered through the figures of seven silver stags, later carried away by barbarians. In the early Christian era, it contained only a few centimetres of water, since immersion was, and is, symbolic.*

The lost loggia of Boniface VIII, *or Pulpitum Bonifacii, shown here in a drawing by Martin van Heemskerck, was linked to the Patriarchate by a series of blind arches.*

Pope Hilarius in the fifth century for the use of 'the people of God', as the inscription tells us. The third chapel, originally dedicated to the Holy Cross, but now to Sts Rufina and Secunda and Sts Cyprian and Justina, is architecturally the most important. It contains a fifth-century mosaic and above the door, a *Crucifixion* in high relief, of the school of Bregno (1492). A fourth chapel, now dedicated to St Venantius, was added by John IV (640–642) in the seventh century, and still has its magnificent sixteenth-century wooden ceiling.

It was perhaps these two chapels, built in honour of St John the Baptist and St John the Evangelist, that later gave the adjoining basilica, originally dedicated to the Saviour, its present name. The Baptistery was called 'St John *ad vestes et ad fontem',* words that refer to the baptismal ritual: *vestes* to the neophytes' white robes, *fontem* to the water in which the catechumens were immersed.

Paul III (1534–1549) had the dome, which was dilapidated, demolished, and the present lantern, with its sloping roof, built.

The Lateran Palace, built on the site of the ancient Patriarchate, was the papal residence from the time of Constantine until the flight to Avignon (1305) and was destroyed, with the basilica, in the fire of 1308. When the Popes returned from Avignon in 1377 they were forced to transfer the Holy See to the Vatican. Then in 1586, Sixtus V (Peretti) had Domenico Fontana demolish almost all that remained of the old fabric, comprising the Loggia of Benedictions and a number of venerable medieval chapels attached to the basilica, in order to build a summer palace for the papal court. Only Constantine's basilica, the early Christian baptistery and the most significant medieval chapel, the Sancta Sanctorum ('Holy of Holies'), were preserved.

The Patriarchate had consisted of a group of buildings that extended as far as Pope Leo's *triclinium*, or dining room, and were joined to the oratory of St Lawrence, called the Sancta Sanctorum. Facing the palace stood the equestrian statue of Marcus Aurelius, which Sixtus IV had returned to that spot. In the portico was an oratory dedicated by Pope John XXII to St Thomas for use as a papal sacristy, in which numerous relics were housed. From the right-hand nave of the church a grand staircase led to the council chamber, which was the same length as the modern front of the palace of Sixtus V, with ten apses, and a dais at the back. On the side facing the piazza to the north, the chamber ended in a covered loggia, built by Boniface VIII for the great Jubilee of 1300. On the wall of this loggia Giotto painted the imposing fresco of which a fragment was placed inside the church and now forms part of Pope Boniface's monument.

The principal entrance to the great palace faced the Chapel of the Sancta Sanctorum, which housed a great number of relics, and from where a magnificent stair, covered by an imposing vault, led to the central part of the palace. There, on the right, stood the tower of Zacharias, near which was another entrance to the palace, in the form of three staircases (the middle one being the Scala Santa), leading to the oratory of St Sylvester and then to that of St Lawrence.

In a lunette in the Vatican Library Cesare Nebbia (1585–1590) painted the scene at the ceremony of the Jubilee promulgated by Sixtus V in the same place as that of Boniface VIII. Since the old Patriarchate disappeared shortly

Pope Sixtus V
had the Loggia of Benedictions demolished.

The city plan

drawn up by Domenico Fontana was actually a plan for developing the whole south-eastern section of the city. Every element in it was connected by a set of logical links: Via Merulana, drawn in a straight line in 1575, could not but end at that point, and at that angle. The great main street of the area had to go through the narrow gap between the men's and women's hospitals. The Loggia of Benedictions, against the façade of the north transept, had to be aligned with it and preserve the ninety-degree angle with the axis of the transept. The palace, therefore, had to be a rectangular block within a square court, at right angles to and parallel with the axes of the basilica, and with the façades of the transept and the basilica of Constantine forming its ends.

The ceiling of the Hall of the Seasons, *which was probably the throne room.*

Loggia of the piano nobile, *which extends on three sides and was the area set aside for the Pope's private apartments.*

afterwards, this picture is the only precious evidence we have of it. In it can be seen the side façade of the basilica, without the porticos that later covered it. On the left is the palace with the council chamber built by Leo III (its side apses can be seen), and outside one can pick out the *Pulpitum* or loggia of Boniface VIII, with the front of the Patriarchate behind it. To the left is the oratory of St Sylvester, and that of the Scala Santa with its little portico.

Sixtus V himself never concealed the fact that he thought of the Lateran basilica as the leading church in Rome, nor that its papal palace should be refurbished to make it a comfortable and dignified setting for the Curia, suitable to house not only the Consistory but also, for extended periods, the papal administration and the Cardinals. Therefore, in designing the great building of the Lateran Palace, on a square plan and placed against the side of the basilica, Fontana took inspiration from the Palazzo Farnese, completed by Michelangelo. From the aesthetic point of view, it is interesting to note the contrast between the solid wall, with its powerful angular rustication, barely joined to a slender moulded string course, and the open loggia-cum-belvedere, which can be seen rising above the roof with columns in the open and receptive to the varying effects of light and shade. The balustrade, formed of pierced Cosmatesque parapets with a spread-eagle as for a lectern, is enriched by the colour of the different marbles. The functional solution of the centrally aligned column emphasizes the architect's freedom of invention, which is consistent with his overall purpose. From the symbolic point of view, one can see how the ancient Imperial heritage has survived. In fact, the significance of the glorifying arch of the tabernacle that covers the altar, of the canopy, the loggia and the vault of the gallery under which, in late antiquity and the Byzantine period, the Emperor would be seated with inflexible ceremony, is well known. It is interesting to compare the concept of the *Pulpitum Bonifacii* with the Imperial Palace of Constantinople, which overlooked the hippodrome (depicted in a relief at the base of the obelisk of Theodosius).

The loggia of Boniface, from which was read the bull signalling the first Christian Jubilee, was altered under Pius IV, and demolished by Domenico Fontana in 1586, by order of Sixtus V, and replaced by the present north portico.

Sixtus V transferred from the Vatican to the Lateran the most solemn event of the ecclesiastical year: the Easter blessing *urbi et orbi*. The rebuilding of the Lateran was completed in the early summer of 1590, shortly before the Pope died, and it is hard to determine what he intended to do. It is certain, however, that the Lateran was then designated the main ecclesiastical complex in Rome.

The Lateran Treaty.
Since 1929, the year of the famous Lateran Treaty between the Vatican and the Italian State, the Lateran, with the basilicas of St Paul's and Santa Maria Maggiore, enjoys the privilege of being 'extraterritorial', making it part of the Vatican City State.

In the Sistine Hall
of the Vatican Library is a fresco by Cesare Nebbia, c. 1588, showing the new Lateran Palace of Sixtus V. The palace was completed a little before the Pope's death. Only the Constantinian baptistery and the basilica were left out of the reconstruction.

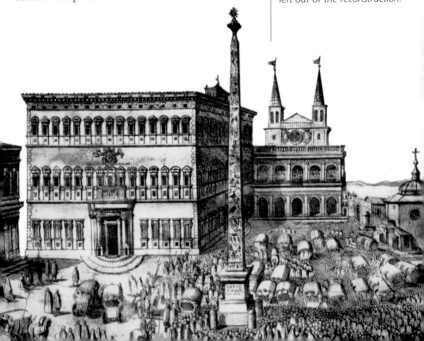

The Scala Santa, situated on the east side of *Piazza San Giovanni in Laterano, is one of the remnants of the old Lateran Palace.*

The Scala Santa and the Sancta Sanctorum

are close by the basilica of St John the Lateran. In 1586, when Sixtus V decided to build the present Lateran Palace, he gave the architect Fontana the task of taking apart the chapel of the Patriarchate and making it more monumental. He also ordered that access to the Sancta Sanctorum should be created by using the grand staircase of the old palace, which consisted of 28 marble steps. From the middle of the fifteenth century it was identified with the stair of the *Praetorium* of Pontius Pilate, the stair climbed by Jesus during his trial; hence its name Scala Santa ('Holy Stair').

The architect completed the operation of moving the Scala Santa to the Sancta Sanctorum in a single night. Ever since then, the Scala Santa and the Sancta Sanctorum, the Christian shrine of shrines, facing the Lateran Palace, have formed a single whole. At the top of the stair, through a small window with a grating, the faithful can just see the old papal chapel where were housed the *acheiropoieta* image of the Saviour ('not made by human hand'), and the most important collection of relics of the Roman martyrs (now in the Vatican Museums). That is what gives the place, the Popes' ancient

private chapel, its sacredness. Entry is via the atrium of the papal chapel, decorated with groups of marble statues, including the *Kiss of Judas* and *Ecce Homo* of Ignazio Jacometti (1854). In the centre, flanked by four other stairs, is the Scala Santa. Those not performing the minor pilgrimage, climbing the stair on their knees, to commemorate Jesus' ascent to be tried before Pontius Pilate, can reach the Sancta Sanctorum by the stair on the right, and go through a bronze door with ancient locks. The chapel was innovative in its architecture and decoration. The walls of its single bay, with a small rectangular apse and a Gothic vault, divided into four by ribs, are partly covered in pieces of ancient marble. The mosaic ceiling of 1278 is a veritable gem of Cosmatesque art. The symbols of the four Evangelists appear in the four sections. On the wall above the altar, the kneeling Nicholas III, flanked by St Peter and St Paul, offers a model of the chapel to Christ enthroned, with two angels.

At the entrance are two scenes showing the martyrdoms of Sts Peter and Paul. In the crucifixion of St Peter, the cross becomes a symbol of contradiction: on the left are the soldiers, on the right the grieving women, and in the background a selection of Roman monuments. The background to the beheading of St Paul is the desolate area of Tre Fontane, with St Paul's church on the right. The blood of Christ thus flows symbolically in the martyrdom of the first of the Apostles, and Rome becomes the New Jerusalem, an image of the divine city. Facing the altar we see the stoning of St Stephen and the martyrdom of St Lawrence, and at the side, the beheading of St Agnes and St Nicholas providing dowries for three poor girls. On each wall, the triangles with lunettes, between the rectangle of the scene and the

The interior has 28 steps, believed to be those climbed by Christ when he appeared before Pontius Pilate.

The papal chapel was built in the time of Constantine and rebuilt by Nicholas III (1277–1281). It was given the name of the Roman martyr St Lawrence, but became known as the Sancta Sanctorum, a pious conflation of the innermost part of the Temple of Jerusalem with the chapel of the Popes. Just as the Holy of Holies of the Old Testament contained the Ark of the Covenant, and was visited once a year by the high priest, the Palatine chapel contained the icon of the Saviour in Majesty, the miraculous *acheiropoieta*, protected by silver doors, and a precious collection of relics of Christ, the Virgin, the Apostles Peter and Paul, and St Agnes. In Rome, as in Jerusalem, no one but the Pope was allowed to officiate in the Sancta Sanctorum, where he performed the evocative Good Friday service.

Only the celebrant was able
to get a complete view of the
canopy above the altar,
where precious relics are still
kept and which refers back
to the Ark of the Covenant
(Exodus 25:22). Similarly, the
porphyry columns and the
architrave have the effect
almost of a pergola. It is a
symbolic visual language that
runs all the way through the
monument, resplendent with
Cosmatesque marble and
described as 'the holiest place
in the entire world' (*Non est
in toto sanctior orbe locus*).

curve of the figure, contain figures of angels,
eight altogether. The rest of the space, at the
sides of the windows, is occupied by large
vases, from which emerge the stems of plants,
curled into three spirals. On the lower level,
around the walls, are 28 niches containing
standing figures from the time of Sixtus. They
represent the Virgin, the Apostles and saints.
On the wall of the altar, two niches, protected by
a grating, give the effect of a reliquary.

Two porphyry columns support the architrave
of the choir, which bears the inscription *Non
est in toto sanctior orbe locus* ('There is no
holier place in the whole world'), marking the
sanctity of the spot, and framing the miraculous (*acheiropoeita*) image of the Saviour,
placed behind the altar inside a reliquary in silver with relief figures, made in the time of
Innocent III. This icon, said to be a true image
of the Saviour, traditionally started by St Luke
and completed by an angel, was the holiest of
those in Rome. Every year, on 15 August, and
also at times of great calamity, the Popes would
carry it in procession to Santa Maria Maggiore,
to 'visit' the image of the Virgin, the *Salus
populi Romani*. Four silver lamps burned con-
stantly beside it. Sts Peter and Paul stand on
either side and in the next lunettes, Sts Agnes
and Lawrence; Sts Nicholas and Stephen. Three
lighted lamps are depicted on the west wall. A
shield bearing a bust of Christ appears in the
mosaic of the little vault, gloriously supported
by four flying angels. Under the canopy is an
altar still preserving precious relics which, with
the *acheiropoeita,* make this papal chapel the
holiest sanctuary of any in the Western world.

*St Lawrence, Roman mar-
tyr, painted here by
Bernardo Strozzi. The papal
chapel named after him is
also known as the Sancta
Sanctorum.*

 NUM CORPUS (Ephesians 4:4)

One body in Christ

Spiritual Message

If there is one characteristic which highlights the great mystery of the Church, it is unity. Unity seen not as a secondary attribute, but as being the centre of mission and history. 'God wills the Church, because he wills unity, and unity is an expression of the depth of his agape' (Ut Unum Sint, 9).

It is the same as the prayer of Christ: 'Father, may they all be one' (John 17:21). It is worthwhile to have a look at the way the first Christian community lived: 'they were one in heart and soul' (Acts 4:32). 'Even as this broken bread was scattered over the hills, and was gathered together and became one, so let your Church be gathered together from the ends of the earth into your kingdom' (Didache, 9).

What is needed in order to live the experience of an ecumenical community? Above all, one has to work towards the inner conversion without which there cannot be 'true ecumenism' (UR, 7). Conversion means to start again from God, who is not ready to be drawn into insignificant details or cultural prejudices. Ecumenism means attention to dialogue in the search for truth, willingness to be 'one body in Christ' (Ephesians 4:4), ready to share with everybody the gift of universal brotherhood. For all this, 'the Church should enter into dialogue with the world in which it exists and labours. The Church has something to say; the Church has a message to deliver; the Church has something to communicate' (ES, 65). This is the profound meaning of every pilgrimage: to set out on the journey which leads to the discovery of a mature faith which helps each one to be united with others beyond tensions and divisions.

SANTA MARIA MAGGIORE

MARIA ABIIT IN MONTANA (Luke 1:39)

Pilgrims with Mary

Reflection

The year 2000, commemorating the birthday of Jesus Christ, recalls his Mother. Jesus was born a Jew of the Jewish Mary.

Her presence in the Gospels is underplayed, but her role is decisive. As a young girl, she gave her meditated and convinced assent to the angel's annunciation of divine motherhood (Lk 1:26–38). Her joy, shared with her cousin Elizabeth, burst out in the exultant Magnificat (Lk 1:39–55). Perplexed, she questioned her adolescent Son, busy with his Father's business (Lk 2:48–49). She spoke quietly to Jesus, and then to the servants, at the wedding feast in Cana (Jn 2:5). A figure of Israel, she pointed out to Jesus that wine was lacking (that the fullness of joy was not fulfilled). From Mary's trust in Jesus at the wedding (of God with humankind) came the new wine of the new covenant in Christ. In her presence, the novelty of Jesus enters the old covenant. Mary's last word was her silence near the Cross, when the dying Jesus entrusted John to her and her to the beloved disciple who 'from that hour took her into his home' (Jn 19:27). The Mother of God is a model of the Church in the matter of faith, charity and perfect union with Christ' (LG, 23). Pilgrimage must start from Mary, the first human place where the Father entrusted the Son to humankind.

Stained glass window in the façade of Santa Maria Maggiore, Rome

History

This patriarchal basilica, built on the Esquiline hill, stands at the end of Via Merulana, formerly Gregoriana, widened and straightened by Pope Gregory XIII (1572–1585) to link it directly with the Lateran. The church harmoniously combines work of different periods, from Christian antiquity to the Baroque. Consequently, the structure of three naves with columns bearing architraves, and part of the mosaic decoration, are basically the fifth-century originals. The Cosmatesque marble pavement and the Romanesque bell-tower are medieval, the coffered ceiling dates from the Renaissance and the two domes and the external elevations from the Baroque period.

Research carried out from 1966 to 1972 shows that the earliest part of the church goes back to the time of Sixtus III (432–440). The mosaic dedication at the top of the arch reads *Xystus episcopus plebi Dei,* 'Pope Sixtus to the people of God', and building is thought to have been started not earlier than about 420, perhaps by demolishing the church of Pope Liberius, if indeed it was still in existence. However, six metres below the level of the present church were found the remains of a sewer and part of a

The statue of the Virgin and Child, *at the highest point of the façade of Santa Maria Maggiore, the most important of the churches dedicated to the Virgin.*

street, dating from the middle of the first century A.D., set inside a courtyard with a portico, on whose walls, corresponding to the apse of the church, a mural calendar was painted in the third or fourth century. A few fragments survive, showing work done on the farm in each month of the year. In front of the basilica of Sixtus was a four-sided portico (some think it was merely a narthex) reduced to a single portico under Eugenius III (1145–1153), as recorded in an inscription still visible in the right-hand courtyard of the church. The portico was redesigned under Gregory XIII (1572–1585).

Following the building phase under Sixtus, a crypt was added to the church in the seventh century, in which the relics of the Grotto of the Nativity, from Bethlehem, and a fragment of what

The legend of the snow.
According to a legend of which there is no written record until the first half of the thirteenth century, Mary is said to have appeared in 352 to Pope Liberius and to the patrician John, a high-ranking figure. She invited them to build a church on a spot where snow had fallen, although it was midsummer. The incident happened on the night of 5 August, on the Cispian summit of the Esquiline hill itself. This defined the area where the church was to be built, and it was said to have been paid for by John and his wife. To commemorate the event, every year on that date a shower of white petals is made to fall from a hole made for the purpose in the ceiling of the church, during a solemn service. It is also referred to in documents as the 'Liberian' church, or 'St Mary of the Snow', although, since no trace of the structure remains, the precise spot on which Liberius may have built his church is still a matter of dispute. Sources suggest that it was situated 'next to the market of Livia', which can actually be located, outside the Esquiline Gate, near the Arch of Gallienus, which is still preserved today.

The basilica of Santa Maria Maggiore, in an eighteenth-century print.

The Confessio
was rebuilt in 1864 by V. Vespignani, with a silver urn by L. Valadier to contain the relics held to be those of the crib of Bethlehem (in the photograph).

was traditionally held to be Jesus' cradle are supposed to have been preserved. For these reasons, until the Carolingian era the basilica was also known as St Mary of the Crib. Pope Paschal I (817–824) had the sanctuary made higher. It was previously the same height as the naves, from which it was divided only by screens. Nicholas IV had a polygonal apse built between 1288 and 1292, further back than the existing one, and a transept; so what was previously the arch of the apse became a triumphal arch. In 1673, under Pope Clement X (1670–1676), Carlo Rainaldi remodelled the exterior of the apse, and between 1740 and 1750, at the behest of Benedict XIV (1740–1758), Ferdinando Fuga added a new façade, linking it with the medieval mosaic façade.

'The mosaics of Santa Maria Maggiore – the arch, the nave and the frieze on the entablature – form one of the supreme examples of fifth-century art' (L. Barroero). They are the oldest surviving iconographic cycle from an early Christian place of worship.

The dominant theme of the mosaics in the triumphal arch is the mystery of the Incarnation of Christ, showing episodes relating to the birth and childhood of the Saviour, taken from the canonical Gospels and also from apocryphal texts. In addition, episodes from the Old

CHRONOLOGY

300–500		600–700	800–1100	
420 *Work probably started*	**432–440** *Sixtus III completes the church*		**1075** *Pope Gregory VII abducted by his opponents while celebrating Christmas Mass in the basilica*	
352 *The Virgin appears to Pope Liberius and invites him to build the church*		**600** *The chapel containing the relics of the Bethlehem Grotto added*	**817–824** *Paschal I has the sanctuary raised*	**1288–1292** *Nicholas IV adds the apse and the transept*

Testament, portrayed in the central nave, present events from the lives of the great patriarchs and precursors of Christ, and thus have a connection with the main theme of the Incarnation. The theme of devotion to the crib was repeated in the now lost oratory next to it, intended to reproduce the setting of Christ's birth, and in a notable *Nativity* by the sculptor Arnolfo di Cambio.

Another dominant idea, especially in the original decoration of the apse, of which the arch survives, is the Divine Motherhood of Mary, proclaimed at the Council of Ephesus in 431. Santa Maria Maggiore was one of the first churches to be dedicated to the Virgin after that date. The intention was to reveal Mary as the preordained instrument of the Incarnation of the Saviour; hence the recurrence of this idea, particularly relevant in an age riven by doctrinal controversy.

The three Popes
who contributed to the rebuilding and restoration of the basilica. Gregory XIII (1572–1585) made alterations to the twelfth-century portico; Clement X (1670–1676) had Carlo Rainaldi redesign the outside of the apse; Benedict XIV (1740–1758) commissioned Ferdinando Fuga to design the façade we see today. From left to right: Gregory XIII, *by Lavinia Fontana;* Clement X, School of Algardi; Benedict XIV, *by Pietro Bracci.*

1347 Cola di Rienzo crowned tribune in Rome	1590 The Sistine Chapel of Domenico Fontana completed	1673 Carlo Rainaldi rebuilds the apse
	1400–1500	**1600–1700**
1378 Rebuilding of the bell-tower completed in the papacy of Gregory XI		1743 Ferdinando Fuga adds the façade, on the orders of Benedict XIV

Art and Architecture

PRACTICAL INFORMATION
Piazza di Santa
Maria Maggiore.
C 06 48 31 95.
▦ 4, 16, 27, 70, 71, 714 to
Piazza di Santa Maria
Maggiore, and many
others to Piazza dei
Cinquecento. **▦** 14.
M Termini, Cavour.
Opening hours
7 a.m.–8 p.m. (to 7 p.m.,
October–March). Last
admissions 15 minutes
before closing time.
✝ **▣**

Ferdinando Fuga's dramatic façade, with five openings in the portico and three in the loggia, includes both the medieval elevation and the central part of the mosaics of Filippo Rusuti, executed at the end of the thirteenth century and depicting Christ enthroned, blessing, in a shield supported by angels, the Virgin and saints on the left, and other saints on the right. In the lower tier, various incidents from the Miracle of the Snow, with Pope Liberius and John the patrician, are depicted on panels bearing captions. Of the three entrances in the façade, the one on the left is the Holy Door, opened only, like those in the three other principal basilicas, on the occasion of a Jubilee.

Four large angels, in marble and gilded bronze, made by Pietro Bracci in 1749, and originally placed on top of the canopy above the altar, are now situated on top of the loggia. On the outside of the façade are various eighteenth-century statues of saints and Popes, in addition to the Madonna and Child. The reliefs decorating the portico, inspired by events connected with the basilica, are also from the first half of the eighteenth century.

The interior, which measures approximately 70 by 35 metres, is harmonious. Its three naves are divided by 40 Ionic columns with capitals standardized by Fuga; they were previously different one from another, like their bases. It was originally lit by many windows, some of them closed up in the sixteenth century. In the spaces created between them, late Mannerist frescoes were painted, showing stories of the Virgin and Christ.

Above the architrave, decorated with a stucco frieze and mosaics of the era of Sixtus III, are 36 fifth-century mosaic panels along both walls, showing scenes from the Old

The Roman obelisk
*in the Egyptian style, in
Piazza dell'Esquilino, was
erected in 1587 by Pope
Sixtus V as a landmark
for pilgrims.*

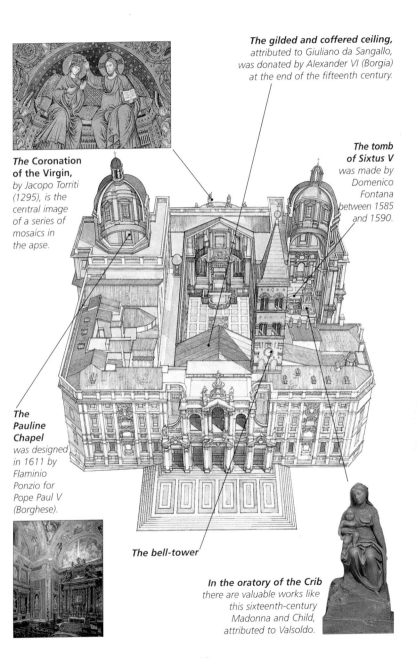

The gilded and coffered ceiling, attributed to Giuliano da Sangallo, was donated by Alexander VI (Borgia) at the end of the fifteenth century.

The Coronation of the Virgin, by Jacopo Torriti (1295), is the central image of a series of mosaics in the apse.

The tomb of Sixtus V was made by Domenico Fontana between 1585 and 1590.

The Pauline Chapel was designed in 1611 by Flaminio Ponzio for Pope Paul V (Borghese).

The bell-tower

In the oratory of the Crib there are valuable works like this sixteenth-century Madonna and Child, attributed to Valsoldo.

The dome of the Sistine Chapel was built by Domenico Fontana in 1586 at the behest of Pope Sixtus V.

Testament, which were framed by small stucco shrines with a tympanum above them. Some of the panels were heavily restored in paint, others reconstructed in 1593 and later. Six were lost at the end of the sixteenth century, to make the large entrance arches to the Pauline and Sistine chapels. Without following a precise logical order, scenes drawn from the stories of Abraham, Isaac and Jacob, in a style that still shows classical influences, are depicted on the left, and from those of Moses and Joshua on the right. The gilded and coffered ceiling, which Vasari considered the work of Giuliano da Sangallo, was donated by Alexander VI (Borgia) at the turn of the fifteenth century. Tradition has it that it used the first gold brought from America by Columbus and given to the King and Queen of Spain. It replaces the original trussed roof, and its decoration was sensitively re-touched in the eighteenth century.

Part of the pavement is the Cosmatesque original, a gift of the Roman aristocrats Giovanni and Scoto Paparoni during the papacy of Eugenius III (1145–1153). The Pauline, or Borghese, Chapel was planned by Flaminio Ponzio between 1605 and 1615 for Pope Paul V. It was built in the area occupied by the old sacristy, with its entrance from the left-hand nave. It is a Greek cross, with pictorial decoration executed between 1610 and 1612, by various artists, including the Cavalier d'Arpino and Guido Reni. On the altar is the venerated image of the Madonna 'Salvation of the Roman People' *(Salus populi Romani),* painted by a Byzantine artist of uncertain date and traditionally attributed to St Luke. Pope Clement VIII and Pope Paul V are buried here, and members of the Borghese family in the crypt below. Two smaller chapels are dedicated to St Charles and St Frances of Rome. Next to it is the oval Sforza Chapel, completed by Giacomo Della Porta in 1573 to a design by Michelangelo. Of almost the same date is the Cesi Chapel, possibly by Guidetto Guidetti, which can be dated to 1550, containing funerary monuments by Guglielmo Della Porta. Benedict XV had the monument to the Queen of Peace erected in the same nave.

In the semicircle of the apse, lit by four flared windows, a mosaic made by Jacopo Torriti between 1288 and 1292, showing the coronation of the Virgin by Christ, on a blue tondo with stars, in front of a row of angels, stands out. Among the donors are Pope Nicholas IV, on the left, and Jacopo Colonna, on the right, with saints. Among them, we note St Francis, intended to be associated with Nicholas, who was the first Franciscan Pope.

Christ enthroned among angels forms part of the mosaics of the façade, created by Filippo Rusuti at the end of the thirteenth century, and frequently restored since.

The interior of the basilica, divided into three naves by 40 Ionic columns, boasts a precious marble Cosmatesque pavement and a Renaissance coffered ceiling.

In the spaces between the windows appear scenes taken from the life of Mary, from the end of the sixteenth century.

The mosaic on the arch of the apse was restored in the twentieth century. It shows the 24 elders of the Apocalypse adoring the Lamb of God, and the emblematic cities of Jerusalem and Bethlehem. In the transept are frescoes, partially revealed in 1931, with images of the prophets in medallions, attributed to Pietro Cavallini, Cimabue, Filippo Rusuti and the young Giotto.

On the present triumphal arch, on the other hand, the mosaic showing scenes from the childhood of Jesus is composed very freely, in rich colouring: the tesserae are of 190 distinct shades. The Nativity as such is not shown, but one can see the Annunciation, with Mary enthroned, spinning purple wool (an apocryphal tradition), the Presentation in the Temple, the Gifts of the Magi, the angel appearing to St Joseph in a dream, a representation of the Governor Afrodisius receiving the Holy Family on the Flight into Egypt, in the city of Sotine, taken from Pseudo-Matthew, the Massacre of the Innocents and the Magi before Herod. At the top of the arch, the empty throne of Christ (*hetoimasia* in Greek) refers to the Second Coming of the Redeemer, on the Day of Judgement.

In the sanctuary, the canopy by Ferdinando Fuga (c. 1740) has columns of porphyry and bronze. A stair leads to the Confessio, made in the second half of the nineteenth century by Virginio Vespignani. On the altar is kept the silver and crystal urn containing the supposed relics of the cradle from Bethlehem. In front of it is a statue of Pius IX at prayer, dating from 1883. Among the

The bell-tower is the highest in Rome, at 75 metres. Romanesque in style, with polychromatic decoration, it was rebuilt in 1370–1378, during the papacy of Gregory XI, on existing foundations. It has been considerably altered over the centuries, and in the sixteenth century a pyramidal spire was added.

funerary monuments, that of Clement IX, in the right nave, from 1671, and that of Nicholas IV, designed by Domenico Fontana in the mid-sixteenth century, are noteworthy.

From the right nave, facing the Pauline Chapel, one reaches the Sistine Chapel, or Chapel of the Blessed Sacrament, executed by Domenico Fontana between 1584 and 1590, for Sixtus V, on the plan of a Greek cross, with a large central dome, two small side chapels and the Pope's tomb. The marble decoration on the walls comes from a classical monument of the time of Severus, the Septizodium, a monumental façade situated at the foot of the Palatine hill.

The canopy, dating from c. 1740, is supported by columns of red porphyry, and is by Ferdinando Fuga.

On side walls respectively are the funerary monuments of Sixtus V and Pius V (the 'victor' at the battle of Lepanto, to mark which he promulgated the short prayer *Maria, Auxilium Christianorum*), to the right and left respectively, also by Fontana. The pictorial decoration is for the most part late Mannerist.

The statues of the three Magi form part of the Nativity of 1289, by the sculptor Arnolfo di Cambio.

In the centre, a little stair leads to the oratory of the Crib, restored by Arnolfo di Cambio in 1289 and brought here in 1590 from the first crypt, which was probably behind the apse or near the sanctuary, by Domenico Fontana. However, he wished to preserve the original setting, which was intended to evoke the Grotto in Bethlehem. Inside, the figures of the prophets David and Isaiah, on the pinnacles of the arch at the entrance, are attributed to Arnolfo, as are the figures of the Nativity – the three Magi, St Joseph, the ox and the ass – except for the Madonna and Child, who are in a niche.

Arnolfo's work forms part of the projects initiated by Nicholas IV and Cardinal Jacopo Colonna. On the pavement, next to the columns of the

The baptistery dates from the early 1600s, but owes its present appearance to the nineteenth-century work of Giuseppe Valadier. A high relief of the Assumption, by Pietro Bernini, adorns the altar.

central nave, can be seen the simple tombstone of the Bernini family, under which also lies the famous Neapolitan architect, sculptor and painter, Gian Lorenzo Bernini.

On the right wall, near the right-hand entrance to the transept, can be seen the Gothic tomb of Cardinal Consalvo Rodríguez, of 1299, with noteworthy Cosmatesque decoration by Giovanni di Cosma, and, in a trilobate arch, a mosaic of the Madonna with saints. From the right-hand nave again, one reaches the baptistery, formerly the Chapel of the Winter Choir, built in 1605 to a design by Flaminio Ponzio, but redesigned in 1825 by Giuseppe Valadier.

Noteworthy among the funerary monuments in this area is that of Odoardo Santarelli, by Alessandro Algardi, which can be dated c. 1640. From the right-hand side one enters the Sacristy of the Canons, with frescoes by Passignano, from 1608.

From here one enters the Chapter House, previously the 'Hall of the Washbasin', with fifteenth-century reliefs, brought here from the demolished papal altar by Mino del Reame.

From the baptistery one can also enter the fifteenth-century Chapel of St Michael and St Peter in Vincoli, with the arms of Cardinal Guillaume d'Estouteville, and a pavement in Cosmatesque style. The surviving fragmentary frescoes have been attributed to Piero della Francesca.

Two palaces flank the basilica, the one on the right built in 1605 by Flaminio Ponzio, under Paul V. The one on the left, which imitates it in style, is later, completed by Fuga in 1735.

CCEPIT EAM DISCIPULUS
IN SUA (John 19:27)

Welcoming Mary

Spiritual Message

The fact that in Jesus Christ God has become man is certainly a unique event. No religion announces a God like this. This is the good news and the beauty of Christianity: it is right to contemplate this mystery. Jesus Christ in his earthly experience tells us how near God is to our own story and, as a result, how great is the dignity that each one has, even the poorest and most abandoned.

God revealed by Jesus Christ is the foundation stone of humanity's greatness and the hope that its existence is not a useless journey. But there is more. If Jesus were only a man, not God, there is no reason to believe in him. The Christian would be living an illusion, without either hope of being redeemed from sin, or the possibility of finding an authentic meaning for life. Only in Jesus, God made man, does there exist the certainty of salvation and freedom. No other man or woman can ever be authentically human without meeting Jesus.

But how is all this possible? It is the same question that Mary put to the angel in the moment of the Annunciation. The answer was just as perplexing as the news it carried. 'Let it be done unto me according to your word' (Luke 1:38). Yes, it is possible to believe in a God who is in love with humanity; it is possible to risk everything for Christ, it is he who holds life's full meaning. It could only be a 'yes' that made Mary the Mother of God and the image of the Church (Luke 1:38). 'Behold your Mother', said Jesus, and John, 'the disciple whom he loved, took her to his own house' (John 19:26–27) and 'brings her into everything that makes up his inner life, that is to say, into his human and Christian "I"' (RMa, 45).

IV

THE BASILICAS OF SANTA CROCE AND SAN LORENZO

I QUIS VULT ME SEQUI, TOLLAT CRUCEM SUAM (Mark 8:34)

If any want to become my followers, let them take up their cross

Spiritual Introduction

There is no human gain without suffering. Christ's cross is written at the bottom of every conscience. But Jesus asks for awareness, not only suffering. For suffering to be salvific, it must be lived with and in Jesus. The cross is not discomfort and hard fate, but the suffering that we endure because of our attachment to Jesus Christ. It is not a casual, but a necessary, suffering. It is not the suffering inherent in our normal existence, but the suffering that depends on the fact that we are Christians' (D. Bonhoeffer).

The act of following Christ passes through the cross. This means self-denial, adhesion to him, communion of life with him. Denying oneself is choosing poverty, taking up one's cross (Mk 8:34) and openness to the purification of suffering that regenerates. It means penetrating the salvific passion of Jesus Christ, which precedes Easter.

Christian life is happy. It is not easy. It means struggling against sin to welcome the Lord Jesus. In him and out of love, God shared in every human suffering up to death. He made it a meaningful instrument of salvation.

The Way to Calvary, by Raphael, Prado, Madrid

Jesus' words bring hope and consolation: 'And when I am lifted up from the earth, I shall draw all people to myself' (Jn 12:32). We can accept suffering only if we are drawn to him. Thus the Christian is baptized into the death of Christ, crucified with him, so as to rise again with him to new life in the Spirit (Rom 6:3–6). We can carry our cross with joy, or at least resignation, and hope only if we entrust ourselves to the Father, so that he may associate us with the way of redemption travelled by the Son.

'Each time suffering befalls us, we can truly say that the universe… the beauty of the world, creation's obedience to God enter our body. And so, why not bless with the most tender gratitude Love who sends us this gift?' (Simone Weil).

SANTA CROCE
IN GERUSALEMME

XALTATUS A TERRA, OMNIA TRAHAM
AD ME IPSUM (John 12:32)

*When I am lifted up from the earth, I
will draw all people to myself*

Reflection

*Church historians of the fourth and fifth centuries record
that while visiting Jerusalem, Helena (mother of the Emperor
Constantine), who died in 326, found on Calvary the wood
of the cross on which Christ was crucified. It was discovered
while work was in progress on constructing the two basilicas,
the Anastasis (the cave of the Holy Sepulchre) and the
Martyrion (the place of crucifixion), built by order of
Constantine and consecrated on 14 September 325. Helena
left part of the Cross in Jerusalem, sent part to Constantinople
and took the rest to Rome, with other relics of the Passion
and some earth from Calvary. They were used in the
construction of the Basilica Sessoriana, giving it the name
'Hierusalem', later Santa Croce in Gerusalemme. Two
inscriptions from the beginning of the fourth century, found
near the church, would seem to confirm Helena's interest in
the site. The relics of the Passion, buried for over a thousand
years in the wall of a chapel dedicated to St Helena, built
half underground, were then transferred to a space above
the right-hand stair and finally, in the 1930s, to the modern
chapel on the left-hand side of the sanctuary. On 11
November 1997 they were moved to the new reliquary,
placed on the altar of the chapel, in a marble tabernacle.*

*The feast of the Cross is celebrated every year on 14
September, under the title 'Exaltation of the Holy Cross', and*

The Reliquary of the Cross, Santa Croce in Gerusalemme, Rome

is one of the most important festivals of the Orthodox Church. From the Adoration of the Cross, celebrated in Santa Croce in Gerusalemme and the Lateran basilica of the Saviour, the Western Church took the ritual of the Veneration of the Cross associated with Good Friday.

'He who does not wish to take up his cross himself loses communion with Christ, and is not his disciple. But he who, following Christ, carries the cross and loses his life, will find it again simply through following Christ and in communion with his cross. The opposite of following Jesus is to be ashamed of him, ashamed of the cross, scandalized by the cross. To follow Jesus means to bind oneself to him in his passion. For this reason the sorrow of Christians is not something to be wondered at; it is, rather, grace and perfect joy' (D. Bonhoeffer).

This is the divine wisdom of the Cross spoken of by the Apostle Paul (1 Corinthians 1:18–25).

History, Art and Architecture

PRACTICAL INFORMATION
12 Piazza di Santa Croce
in Gerusalemme.
06 701 47 69.
9. 30b.
Opening hours 7 a.m.–
7 p.m.

Statue of St Helena
*in Santa Croce. Two
inscriptions in her honour,
dating from the beginning
of the fourth century and
found near the church,
confirm that she had a
residence there.*

The basilica stands on the slopes of the Esquiline hill, a place rich in history and associated with meditation on Christ's Passion. It was founded by Constantine the Great and his mother, St Helena, on a site occupied by an Imperial palace, called the 'Sessorianum', perhaps signifying 'auditorium', during the pontificate of St Sylvester I (314–337). Although it was called the Basilica of Helena or Basilica Sessoriana, its official name was the Hierusalem. The name referred specifically to the relic of the Cross and the other relics of the Passion of Our Lord, miraculously discovered on Calvary and brought to Rome by the Emperor's aged mother. But it also links Rome with Jerusalem, an association reinforced by the crucifixion of St Peter.

However, the name Santa Croce in Gerusalemme was adopted in the later Middle

**Santa Croce in
Gerusalemme,**
*façade commissioned by
Pope Benedict XIV (1743).*

Ages. According to tradition, Pope Gregory the Great appointed a Cardinal priest incumbent of the basilica, and over the centuries it was renovated several times, for example under Popes Gregory II (715–731) and Adrian I (771–795).

The funerary inscription of Pope Benedict VII (975–984), beside the main entrance, says that because the church was so rich in relics, a set of buildings designed to house canons was constructed alongside it. No canons were appointed, however, and in 1049 Pope Leo IX placed it in the hands of the Benedictines of Monte Cassino. When they moved to San Sebastiano in 1062, Pope Alexander II installed the canons regular of San Frediano of Lucca and in the reign of Pope Lucius II (1144–1145), they rebuilt the basilica in the Romanesque style. They created three naves, added a campanile with double- and triple-arched

Hemisphere of the apse.
Detail of the cycle of frescoes showing the Finding of the Cross: The Cross of Christ captured by Chosroes.

'If something good loses its savour, then turn at once to the Crucifixion (...) and study the crown of thorns, the nails, the spear between his ribs. Gaze upon the wounds in his feet and his hands, on his head, in his side, his whole body. Remember how much he loved you who so suffered for you, who endured so much for you, who bore so much for you. Believe me, who seeing such a thing, found all things joyful (...) by virtue of the passion of Christ' (St Bonaventure, 'On the Perfect Religious Life' in Five Mystical Works).

The Titulus,
one of the relics preserved in Santa Croce, carries the inscription 'Jesus of Nazareth King of the Jews'.

'When you were buried with him in baptism, you were also raised with him through faith in the power of God, who raised him from the dead' (Colossians 2:12).

openings and built a portico in front of the fourth-century façade.

The whole complex remained deserted throughout the Avignon papacy, until Pope Urban V handed it over to the Carthusians about 1370. They in turn carried out important restoration work, mainly while the Spanish Cardinal priests Pedro Gonzales de Mendoza (1484–1493) and López de Carvajal (1495–1523) were incumbents of the basilica.

In 1561, after the Carthusians were transferred to Santa Maria degli Angeli, in the Baths of Diocletian, Lombard Cistercians from the congregation of San Bernardo took over. They are still in charge of the basilica. One of their first projects, under Cardinal Francisco Pacheco, was the construction in 1570 of the Chapel of the Relics, and Pomarancio was commissioned to paint a series of frescoes of the story of the Finding of the Cross, in the Chapel of St Helena.

Santa Croce's present appearance is the result of its rebuilding as a Baroque church between 1741 and 1744 at the behest of Pope Benedict XIV Lambertini, under the direction of two architects, Domenico Gregorini, from Rome, and the

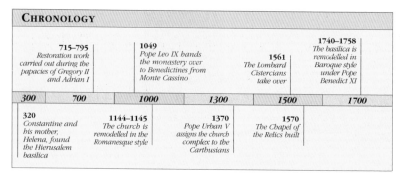

CHRONOLOGY

300	700	1000	1300	1500	1700
	715–795 *Restoration work carried out during the papacies of Gregory II and Adrian I*	**1049** *Pope Leo IX hands the monastery over to Benedictines from Monte Cassino*		**1561** *The Lombard Cistercians take over*	**1740–1758** *The basilica is remodelled in Baroque style under Pope Benedict XI*
320 *Constantine and his mother, Helena, found the Hierusalem basilica*		**1144–1145** *The church is remodelled in the Romanesque style*	**1370** *Pope Urban V assigns the church complex to the Carthusians*	**1570** *The Chapel of the Relics built*	

Sicilian Pietro Passalacqua. Town planning works were also carried out at the same time. Monte Cipollaro was levelled, and roads linking Santa Maria Maggiore, St John Lateran and Santa Croce, which stands at the end of the axis of Via Felice, built by order of Pope Sixtus V at the end of the sixteenth century, were completed.

The prestigious Sessorian Library, housed in an imposing gallery built between 1724 and 1727 by the architect Sebastiano Cipriani, with frescoes by the painter Gian Paolo Pannini, of Piacenza, belongs to the monastery.

Until 1871, when it was taken over by the Italian state, the library held the famous Fondo Sessoriano, a collection now in the National Central Library in Rome. It consisted of over 450 valuable manuscripts and printed books, and was founded by Abbot Ilarione Rancati in the middle of the seventeenth century.

In 1570, on the authority of Pius V, the relics were moved from the underground chapel of St Helena to a place above, to preserve them from damp. Because of the increasing numbers of pilgrims, it was decided to build the present chapel, using the former sacristy. It was designed by Florestano Di Fausto, inaugurated in 1930 and finished in 1952. In the photograph, the Chapel of the Relics.

The high altar
of Santa Croce expresses the link between the celebration of the Eucharist and the sacrifice of Good Friday.

The Relics.
In addition to relics with a more ancient pedigree (three fragments of the Cross, a nail from the crucifixion, the Titulus and two thorns from Christ's crown), other relics, all deemed to support teaching about the Passion, are preserved in the basilica. They include the horizontal limb of the cross of the Good Thief, St Dismas, a joint from the finger of St Thomas and fragments of the pillar of the scourging, the Grotto of the Crib and the Holy Sepulchre. In early days, the list of this type of relics also included a coin which belonged to Judas, the sponge soaked in vinegar and the rock on which Christ sat when he pardoned Mary Magdalene. In the photograph: the Reliquary of the Cross.

The present façade, dramatic and full of movement, replaces the old medieval one. Sets of pilaster strips divide it into three concave and convex bays, under a curved pediment surmounted by a decorative tympanum, and by balusters and statues. Below, three doors open into an oval atrium with a domed vault, its surrounding ambulatory decorated with groups of pilaster strips and columns. Eight ancient granite columns, four on each side, alternate with six pilasters dating from the eighteenth-century renovation, dividing the interior into three naves. On the wooden false vault that carries the arms of Pope Benedict XIV is a painting, *St Helena Ascending into Heaven*, by Corrado Giaquinto, dated 1744. In the sanctuary there is an eighteenth-century baldacchino, and below the high altar a fine basalt urn containing the remains of Sts Caesarius and Anastasius. Another painting by Giaquinto, *Apparition of the Cross on the Day of Judgement*, is in the vault. The semicircular apse has a cycle of frescoes of the Holy Cross found by St Helena and recovered by Heraclius, and above them, within a mandorla formed of cherubim, one of *Christ Blessing*, attributed to Antoniazzo Romano and dated 1492. Also worth noting are the Romanesque frescoes in the gable, a twelfth-century Cosmatesque pavement, and seventeenth- and eighteenth-century paintings

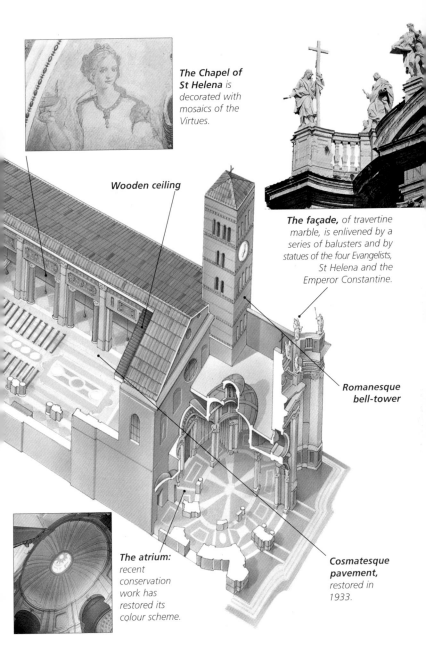

The Chapel of St Helena is decorated with mosaics of the Virtues.

Wooden ceiling

The façade, of travertine marble, is enlivened by a series of balusters and by statues of the four Evangelists, St Helena and the Emperor Constantine.

Romanesque bell-tower

The atrium: recent conservation work has restored its colour scheme.

Cosmatesque pavement, restored in 1933.

The Cosmatesque
pavement inside the church.

'The Son of God came down into the world and became flesh, he suffered on the cross, he has redeemed us from our imprisonment, he has made glorious our humanity. For God has loved not only the just but also the sinners, and he has sent his Son to die for us that we might burn with ardent love for him. We should love Almighty God because he created us, but even more so because he has redeemed us. We should love him because he has given us being, but even more so because he has saved us through the death of his Son, so that we may enjoy for all eternity the life of the blessed. Let us love God because he loves us' (St Bernard, The Word and the Soul: Daily Meditations).

in the side aisles by Raffaele Vanni, Luigi Garzi, Carlo Maratta and Giuseppe Passeri. The funerary monument of Cardinal Quiñones, erected in the sixteenth century to a design by Jacopo Sansovino, is of interest.

Focal points for pilgrims are the two semi-subterranean chapels linked with the basilica by two flights of steps on either side of the sanctuary, one the entrance, the other the exit. On the right is the Chapel of St Helena, on the left the much later Chapel of the Pietà.

The holy Empress Helena sprinkled earth from Calvary on the floor of the first chapel, which bears her name and is also called the *cubiculum Sanctae Helenae*; then she placed there the precious relic of the Cross. It is known that the Emperor Valentinian III (425–455), with his mother Galla Placidia and his sister Honoria, had the vault decorated with rich mosaics, of which no trace remains. The mosaic was completely renewed at the turn of the sixth century by Baldassare Peruzzi, from a design by Melozzo of Forlì, and since being restored in 1995 it has been revealed in all its glory. In the centre is the figure of Christ blessing, surrounded by the Evangelists and four events from the crucifixion. Frescoes showing the finding of the Cross were painted on the area below the mosaic by Nicolò Circignani, called Pomarancio, in 1590. The statue of St Helena above the altar is a copy of the Vatican Juno, conveniently adapted by the addition of symbols of the Passion. In 1602 Rubens painted three canvases for this chapel: *St Helena with the Holy Cross*, the *Crucifixion* and *Christ Crowned with Thorns*. They were removed in 1724 because they had been damaged by damp, and later sold. They are now in Grasse, in France.

The Chapel of the Pietà, or Gregorian Chapel, was built between 1495 and 1520 in accordance with the wishes of Cardinal Bernardino López de Carvajal, as a mirror image of the Chapel of

St Helena, and joined to it. The name evokes the love of God, and may refer to the pity of God the Father who sacrifices his Son, and of the Son of God who sacrifices himself, or to the pity of humanity, for whom the sacrifice is made, for him who makes it. Divine pity, as an act of grace, is different from human pity, which is a feeling of love or compassion.

The Chapel of the Pietà, to whose altar a marble bas-relief of the dead Christ lying in Mary's lap was added in 1628–1629, is linked with the altar of St Gregory. This is a precious reliquary in the form of a triptych, with a silver frame, doors that open, and some 200 relics. A late thirteenth- or early fourteenth-century mosaic of the *Imago pietatis*, depicting the Suffering Christ, occupies the centre. In the silver frame seven enamels survive, of the ten that were planned. They depict the scourging, Christ carrying the cross, the crucifixion, and the arms of Anjou, the Holy Sepulchre, del Balzo and Orsini Montfort. The work was probably commissioned by Raimondo del Balzo, who went on a pilgrimage to the Holy Land in 1380; it was donated to the basilica in 1386. A few years later, word spread that the image of Christ was the same one seen by Pope

The Pietà.
In Italy this refers to two different images of the dead Christ. One shows him stretched out in Mary's lap (epitomized by the *Pietà* of Michelangelo), with or without St John the Evangelist, Mary Magdalene and other figures. The other, properly called the *Imago pietatis,* shows the bust of the suffering Christ, half or three-quarters of which emerges or rises from the tomb. The head is inclined, the eyes half shut and the hands either open to show their wounds or folded on the lower body or the breast, which bears the marks of the wound made by the spear. The skin is pitted with scars from the scourging. Behind Christ is seen the whole cross, or its horizontal limb. This image gives us a way of recalling to mind the mystery of Christ's suffering, presenting him as the Man of Sorrows. It is an icon of Holy Saturday, and shows Christ's descent into the tomb, the bridegroom who approaches the bridal bed, purifying the Church with his blood and making her worthy to become the Holy and Immaculate Bride of the King of Glory (O BASILEUS TES DOXES IC XC, in the inscription above Christ's head).

The reliquary kept in the Chapel of St Gregory.

Discovery and Triumph of the Cross *(detail), attributed to Antoniazzo Romano.*

'O Domine Iesu Christe, adoro te in cruce pendentem'

('Lord Jesus Christ, I adore you as you hang from the cross'). A prayer said to have been composed by St Gregory after he saw the vision, and recited in private before the image of the Pietà by the devout who had confessed and were contrite. In this way they could earn an enormous number of indulgences, and could also obtain them on behalf of souls in Purgatory, on condition that they had made their confession and followed the prayer with five *Paters* and five *Aves*, gazing always at the image.

Gregory the Great. The inscription *Fuit Sancti Gregorii Magni Papae* can be read on the tympanum of the reliquary. Tradition has it that as St Gregory was celebrating Mass in the Basilica Sessoriana, the Christ in Pietà appeared, in the attitude of the Man of Sorrows. No life of the saint mentions this vision, and the legend is thought to have originated in the basilica itself. An inscription below the *Imago pietatis*, engraved in 1495 by Israel Van Meckenem, supports this suggestion. It reads: 'Copy of the holy image of the Pietà which Pope Gregory the Great caused to be painted in the church of Santa Croce, following his vision'.

St Bernard of Clairvaux (1090–1153) was also blessed with the same vision, while he was celebrating Mass in the oratory near the monastery of Tre Fontane, in Rome. The vision of St Gregory was depicted in 1630 on the vault of the Chapel of the Pietà by two artists, Girolamo Nanni, of Milan, who came to Rome in 1620, and the Roman painter Francesco Nappi (c. 1565–1630). The painting expresses the teaching

114

about Purgatory and how souls may be liberated through the prayers of the faithful who appeal to the saints for intercession. St Gregory and St Bernard, whose spiritual descendants were responsible for managing the chapel in 1561, are both included. In the centre of the vault, starting from the bottom, we see penitent souls enveloped in the flames of Purgatory. On either side, angels choose two who, their penance now at an end, set out to follow the tiny soul rising towards the Holy Trinity. St Gregory the Great, in his papal robes, his tiara beside him, and St Bernard, with his white cowl and his Abbot's mitre, are shown kneeling in the middle section. Standing behind St Gregory we can see St Benedict of Nursia, and behind St Bernard, St Robert of Molesme. Their role is to intercede for souls in Purgatory. Above them are other, more powerful mediators: St Paul and St John the Baptist on the left, St Peter, with the keys of Paradise, and another Apostle, on the right. Between the two pairs of figures is the Virgin, in an attitude of supplication before the Trinity, which crowns the composition, her gaze directed towards Christ. In the four sections of the vault are four symmetrical scenes, two facing St Gregory, two St Bernard.

In keeping with the Catholic doctrine solemnly reaffirmed by the Council of Trent (Decree on Purgatory, 1563), the freeing of souls from Purgatory is linked with the sacrifice of the Eucharist. If this is celebrated at the altar of San Gregorio al Celio the soul enjoys a plenary indulgence and the personal intercession of St Gregory the Great. A few other altars have the same privilege, including the Gregorian altar in Santa Croce, which dates from 1574. The church was included in the pilgrims' itinerary

The representation of Christ Pantocrator *dominates the centre of the vault.*

The **Pietà,** *bas-relief above the altar, by an unknown sculptor of the early seventeenth century.*

The Triumph of the Cross, *painted by Corrado Giaquinto between 1742 and 1743, measures 6 metres by 4.*

Pilgrimages to Santa Croce.

The basilica was much visited by pilgrims, especially at particular times of the liturgical year:
14 September – Exaltation of the Cross;
3 May – Discovery of the Cross;
fourth Sunday in Lent – exposition of the relics;
Good Friday – papal processions from the Lateran to Santa Croce (since the eighth century).

of Roman churches, and later became a Jubilee basilica. In the mid-sixteenth century it was also included in St Philip Neri's route of the Seven Churches and it remains today an important religious site for both Rome and the Universal Church.

'Spend a long time in this church, and reflect that our triumph is in the Cross alone, and that it is our only banner. Rome, city of the martyrs and the Apostles, will perhaps in this church teach you the secret of the greatness of Christianity: the Cross. The rest is mere worldly noise. If you are to find, among the thousand duties of your pilgrimage, and amid the uproar of the modern city, a little quiet and a profound peace, go to one of Rome's churches, to a ruin or a park, and meditate on the fate of the world and on what it is in the world that persists in being worldly. Reflect on your Christian vocation, on the Christian faith, which today is burdened with all the weight of past centuries and with all the possibilities of centuries to come. Rome is the best place for Christian meditation' (written for pilgrims in the 1975 Jubilee Year).

PREDICAMUS CHRISTUM
CRUCIFIXUM (1 Corinthians 1:23)

We preach Christ crucified

Spiritual Message

Faced with all the misery and injustice present in the world today, it is not easy to believe in God who participates in the history of humanity. Yet in the Bible God is presented as Father.

It is the faithful love, unchanging and always new, towards every person. But, then, why suffering, why this immense agony in a world which appears to be far from the best of worlds? This should have been enough to conclude that God is only an idea, if there were not a 'but', expressed through the scandal of the Cross: 'God loved the world so much that he gave his only Son' (John 3:16). He did not 'spare even his own Son, but delivered him up for us all' (Romans 8:32).

Before a God who is not indifferent to what is happening, there is a sense of bewilderment. It is God-with-us that Jesus presents to us. A God who sympathizes with humanity's lot, making himself present to those who have no hope and no dignity.

The Cross is 'folly' which cannot be understood by 'human wisdom'. God consents to present himself powerless before the person who is conscious of his or her freedom. He manifests an omnipotence which is humbled and nailed. This is the disturbing truth belonging to Good Friday: the God revealed by Jesus Christ is not a passive spectator of humanity's suffering, but is the One who takes it on himself to give it meaning. Recognizing that the Cross is the real sign through which the Son of God manifests himself as the Redeemer of the world, every believer finds the strength to change despair into hope.

It is for this reason that the Church continues to preach 'Christ crucified, the power of God, and the wisdom of God' (1 Corinthians 1:23, 24).

SAN LORENZO

ESTES ESTIS (Luke 24:48)

You are witnesses of Christ

Reflection

'St Lawrence was a deacon of the Church of Rome. He was a minister of the blood of Christ and, for the name of Christ, he shed his blood. He reciprocated what he had received. He loved Christ in his life, he imitated him in his death' (St Augustine, Discourses, *304, 1–2*).

Reliable information about St Lawrence is scarce. It is known that he suffered martyrdom during the persecution of Valerian, four days after the martyrdom of Pope Sixtus II and Lawrence's four fellow-deacons. He was buried in Agro Verano where the basilica of St Lawrence outside the Walls was built during the time of Constantine. Tradition narrates that he died on a gridiron, and art portrays his death thus. His feast was already celebrated in the fourth century. St Ambrose, the first person who cited the passion of St Lawrence, mentioned that Lawrence met Pope Sixtus in chains and asked to be taken along to martyrdom. Instead, Sixtus ordered him to distribute the belongings of the Church in his custody among the poor. When Valerian arrested him and demanded 'the treasures of the Church', Lawrence showed him 'the countless troops' of the city's poor and sick (St Leo the Great, Homilies, *85, 2*). It is said that while he was being martyred, Lawrence prayed at length for Rome. 'The flames that Valerian prepared did not win over the flames of Christian charity, because the fire that burned Lawrence externally was weaker than the

St Lawrence, mosaic, San Lorenzo, Rome

flames that consumed him from within' (St Leo the Great, Homilies, 85, 4). Today, there are other trials of our Christian faith: the convincing persuasion of the permissive life in the West; tacit assent to unjust regimes; the economic inequality that harms two-thirds of humankind; silence before laws that attack life or manipulate it; scarce efforts to wipe out the great wounds caused by poverty: forced prostitution, child labour and sexual exploitation, organ trafficking. Lawrence, the deacon, reminds us all to be Christ's witnesses (Luke 24:48).

History, Art and Architecture

PRACTICAL INFORMATION
3 Piazzale del Verano.
C 06 49 15 11.
71, 492.
19, 19b, 30b.
Opening hours 7 a.m.–
12 p.m., 3.30–6 p.m.
(Summer 7.30 p.m.) 📷 ♿

Lawrence the deacon, a victim of persecution under Valerian and buried in the catacomb of Cyriaca at Verano, on Via Tiburtina, was among the martyrs most venerated in Rome. About 330, Constantine may have erected a small oratory above his tomb, with a double stair to give easier access for pilgrims. It is certain that he also built, at the foot of the hill near the venerated memorial, a large circular cemetery basilica, with curved naves, that was called 'the Great'. Remains

**Funerary monument
of Alcide
De Gasperi**

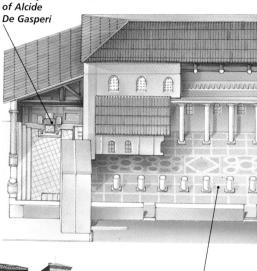

Interior of San Lorenzo

**The Cosmatesque
pavement** *is divided
into three aisles, with
a double row of
eleven columns.*

The façade, *destroyed by bombing
on 16 July 1943, was restored
between 1946 and 1949.*

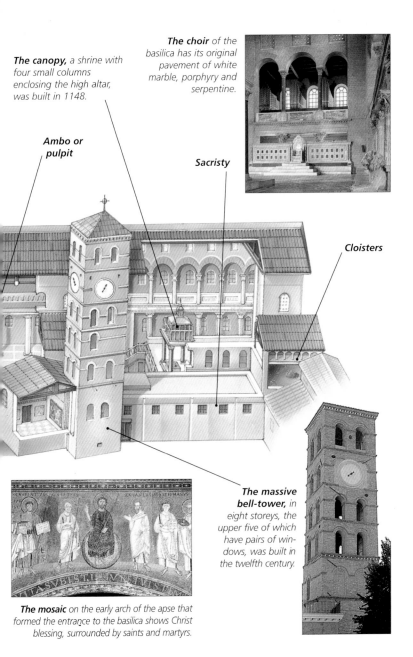

The canopy, a shrine with four small columns enclosing the high altar, was built in 1148.

The choir of the basilica has its original pavement of white marble, porphyry and serpentine.

Ambo or pulpit

Sacristy

Cloisters

The massive bell-tower, in eight storeys, the upper five of which have pairs of windows, was built in the twelfth century.

The mosaic on the early arch of the apse that formed the entrance to the basilica shows Christ blessing, surrounded by saints and martyrs.

of it now lie partly under the modern Verano cemetery. It was not until the second half of the sixth century that Pope Pelagius II (579–590) cut away part of the hill and built a basilica of three naves with internal galleries on the site of the early memorial to the martyr. It was oriented in the opposite direction from the present church, built by Honorius III (1216–1227), to cope with the massive water penetration that was threatening the basilica of Pelagius. Its floor was raised, and it became the sanctuary of the medieval church, which surrounded and enclosed it.

The cloisters, with paired small columns, were probably built by the Cosmati brothers in the twelfth century. The monastery to which they belong was extended in 1190 by the addition of an elegant portico.

This complex of buildings, in the form of two structures facing each other, is preceded by a narthex by Vassalletto. It has a Cosmatesque pavement, and is divided into three naves with a double row of columns, taken from other sites. Two stairs lead to the raised sanctuary, also in three parts, from which can be seen the mosaic that survives from the apsidal arch of Pelagius church. It shows Christ between Sts Peter and Paul, with the martyrs Sts Stephen, Hippolytus and Lawrence, and Pope Pelagius. At the end of the nineteenth century, the funerary chapel of Pius IX was created in the crypt, decorated with mosaics on a gold background. Also noteworthy is the canopy of 1148, signed by the Roman marble workers Giovanni, Pietro, Angelo and Sasso. The sacristy leads to the late twelfth-century cloisters, the work of Clement III, where there is a collection of sculpture and inscriptions.

San Lorenzo, one of the five patriarchal basilicas and one of the Seven Churches on the itinerary of St Philip Neri, suffered serious bomb damage in 1943. Many parts of it were restored between 1946 and 1950.

ISI GRANUM FRUMENTI
MORTUUM FUERIT (John 12:24)

*Unless the grain of wheat falling
into the ground die*

Spiritual Message

*To offer one's own life is a surprising act. The martyr troubles
consciences by giving witness to a unique experience: the
mystery of Christ. What the martyr has seen and heard becomes
part of his or her life, as it was for St Lawrence. Of him St
Augustine wrote: 'He was a deacon of the Church in Rome.
There he was a minister of the blood of Christ and, in Christ's
name, he shed his blood. John the Apostle clearly describes the
mystery of the Last Supper: "As Christ had laid down his life for
us, we ought to lay down our lives for the brethren" (1 John
3:16). Lawrence understood all this. He understood it and put
it into practice ... He loved Christ during his life, he imitated
him in his death' (Discourses, 304, 1–4).*

*But there is another even deeper truth: martyrdom is the
horizon of Christian life, giving meaning to all attitudes and
actions – characterizing the journey of the follower of Christ.
The contradiction which the Gospel leads to seems
unacceptable: 'Amen, amen I say to you, unless the grain of
wheat falling into the ground die, itself remains alone. But if it
die, it brings forth much fruit' (John 12:24–25). Yet the one who
has a reason to die also holds the reason to live: love. A life given
out of love is the greatest challenge to indifference. Following
Jesus is not a sad journey full of suffering, but the discovery of
real freedom and true joy. The martyr proclaims that the last
word is love as a gift of self, and reminds us that believing is the
action that gives meaning to our own being and makes it
possible for the believer to share in the Trinitarian life. 'Christ is
everything for us. If you are in need of help, he is strength. If you
are afraid of death, he is life. If you desire heaven, he is the way.
If you want to get away from darkness, he is the light' (St
Ambrose, On Virginity, 16).*

V

THE MARTYRS' SANCTUARIES
(The catacombs)

BEATI QUI PERSECUTIONEM
PATIUNTUR (Matthew 5:10)

Blessed are those who are persecuted

Spiritual Introduction

Christian life means sharing in the passion and death of Jesus Christ. Without compromises, mitigation, hesitation. It means and requires heroism. It is a hard life, totally put to risk at a high price. Persecution is included in the immense horizon of the Christian adventure.

While the Greek genius is presented as order, harmony, equilibrium, the Christian genius seems to be contradiction, persecution, death: 'Blessed are those who are persecuted' (Matt 5:10), 'Blessed are those who die in the Lord' (Rev 14:13). 'To those who enter its sphere, the cross imposes such an effort of unification that it causes heroic tension on the will. It is necessary to love the enemy, beyond our human nature; it is necessary to do good to those who hate us. It is necessary to learn to hate even our life (John 12:25). Christian life is a complete, generous, personal passage, with no return and no regrets, from classical and human equilibrium to the absence of equilibrium originating from the total contact of man with infinite love' (G. Bevilacqua). But the destination is the joy of the Resurrection.

The Fathers of the Church often attest to the value of the relics of the saints. 'In the body of the saints, there is a certain force, due to the just soul that dwelt in and made use of it for many years' (St Cyril of Jerusalem, Catechesis 18).

The Massacre of the Innocents, by Guido Reni,
National Picture Gallery, Bologna

'Whoever touches the bones of martyrs is capable of participating in their holiness, because of the grace that abides in their bodies' (St Basil, On Psalm 115). St John Chrysostom invites us to visit the tombs of martyrs, which are rich in blessings. St Paulinus of Nola exalts the power of the Relic of the Cross (Letter 3,6). And catacombs are also places of prayer. St Augustine exhorts: 'When you pray, go to your private room, shut yourself in, and so pray to your Father who is in that secret place (Matt 6:6). This room is our heart. Spiritual prayer takes place in the depth of our heart' (The Sermon on the Mount, 3,10–11).

A visit to the catacombs brings Christians back to the origins of their faith. Jesus asks everyone, even those who do not meet obstacles in the profession of their faith, to say a prayer coming from their inmost heart, before becoming a witness in public.

Historical Outline

PRACTICAL INFORMATION
Open 8.30 a.m.–12 p.m.,
2.30 p.m.–5 p.m.
(5.30 summer time).
Admission
adults 8,000 Lire
concessions 4,000 Lire

Tickets include guided
tour. Concessions for:
school parties with a
letter of introduction
from the head teacher;
groups of students on
catechism courses or
preparating for sacra-
ments; children under
15; members of the
armed forces in uniform
or with ID. To arrange
for the celebration of
Mass in the catacombs,
please book by telephone
or fax.

The term 'catacombs' refers to the ancient underground Christian cemeteries.

For health reasons, Roman law prohibited burials within the city walls; so catacombs are always found outside the city. Contrary to a persistent, but false, belief, they were never used by Christians as places in which to hide from persecution. They served only as underground cemeteries, and any gatherings that took place in them would have been connected with burials, or with the cult of the martyrs buried there. Persecutions were limited to specific periods in the history of the Empire: during the reign of Nero (between A.D. 64 and 67), Domitian (in A.D. 96), Decius (249–251), Valerian (253–260) and Diocletian (in the West, principally between 303 and 305).

The oldest clusters of catacombs date from the end of the second and the beginning of the third century. Before that, Christians were buried in the same places as pagans, with no segregated burial zones. As Christian communities

Via Aurelia

Christ the Good Shepherd.
The shepherd carrying a lamb is a figure present in pagan art, from archaic Greece onwards.

Catacombs of St Calixtus, gallery in the first zone ❶
First official cemetery of the Church of Rome.

Catacombs of St Sebastian ❷
In the crypt there is a bust of the saint, attributed to Bernini.

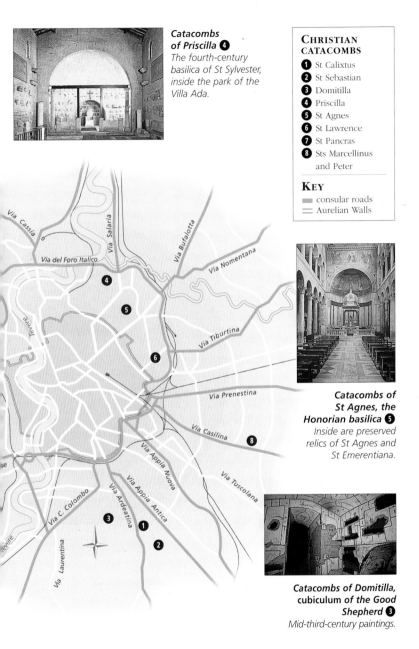

Catacombs of Priscilla ④
The fourth-century basilica of St Sylvester, inside the park of the Villa Ada.

CHRISTIAN CATACOMBS

① St Calixtus
② St Sebastian
③ Domitilla
④ Priscilla
⑤ St Agnes
⑥ St Lawrence
⑦ St Pancras
⑧ Sts Marcellinus and Peter

KEY

▬ consular roads
═ Aurelian Walls

Catacombs of St Agnes, the Honorian basilica ⑤
Inside are preserved relics of St Agnes and St Emerentiana.

Catacombs of Domitilla, cubiculum of the Good Shepherd ③
Mid-third-century paintings.

At the beginning of the fifth century, the custom of burying the dead in the catacombs began to decline, although pilgrims would still visit them as an act of devotion. From the eighth to the ninth century, with the Roman countryside deserted and unsafe because of barbarian incursions, the sanctuaries were gradually abandoned, and the Popes decided to move the venerated tombs to the city. The catacombs were rediscovered in more recent times; they were explored by Antonio Bosio (1575–1629) and later studied by the great Roman archaeologist Giovanni Battista de Rossi (1822–1894). Today the running of the Christian catacombs is entrusted to the Pontificia Commissione di Archeologia Sacra (Papal Commission for Sacred Archaeology), which manages and funds digs and restoration.

Giovanni Battista de Rossi

grew, they needed to create communal cemeteries in order to ensure that all members, however humble, would have a religious burial. Problems of space and the high cost of land were solved by resorting to digging underground, whenever the nature of the rock, which had to be strong yet easy to cut, allowed it. Since Rome was built on a bedrock of soft tufa, this system was widely used, allowing additional burial space to be created by digging several galleries, one on top of another.

The catacombs are a system of long corridors or galleries, whose walls contain dug-out tombs (*loculi* or cells). Air and light entered through vertical square shafts called *lucernari* (skylights). The body would be laid in the cell wrapped in a shroud and the tomb sealed with tiles or marble slabs, on which would be carved the deceased's name and date of death. The latter was called *dies natalis* (birthday), since for Christians, death was the beginning of the afterlife, which is the true life. Opening onto the galleries, besides the cells, were also *arcosolia*: these were loftier tombs, topped by an arch; and family burial chambers, called *cubicula*.

ROME AT THE TIME OF THE EARLY CHRISTIANS

Trajan

Augustus (27 B.C.–A.D. 14)			Vespasian (A.D. 69–79)		Trajan (98–117)	
	Caligula (A.D. 37–41)	Claudius (A.D. 41–54)				

Julio-Claudian Dynasty (27 B.C. – A.D. 68)		Flavian Dynasty (A.D. 69–96)		Antonin

Augustus

	Tiberius (A.D. 14–37)	Nero (A.D. 54–68) First persecution of Christians in A.D. 65. Sts Peter and Paul executed in A.D. 64 or 67	Titus (A.D. 79–81)	Domitian (A.D. 81–96) Christian and Jewish philosophers expelled from Rome in A.D. 93–94	Nerva (A.D. 96–98)	Hadrian (117–138)

A catacomb containing the burial place of a martyr would become particularly famous, and pilgrims would come from all over the Christian world to pay their respects at the venerated tomb.

The tombs of the martyrs have always been well maintained and embellished, in particular by Constantine (306–337) and Pope Damasus (366–384), who wrote his famous inscriptions in verse especially for the martyrs' burial-places.

The cemeteries belonged to the Church, which administered them first through the *fossores*, workmen who specialized in underground digging, and later through the deacons and presbyters of the city's parishes, called *tituli*.

Various special rituals were performed in the catacombs on the anniversaries of the dead. One of them was called the *refrigerium*, or funeral banquet, a pagan custom the Church tolerated within certain limits. The martyrs' anniversaries were also commemorated there, and on those occasions the faithful would gather for the celebration of the Eucharist.

The decoration

was simple, mostly of frescoes, with subjects derived from pagan art used decoratively or symbolically, such as an olive branch, a figure in prayer or a fisherman. What was really novel was the use of subjects from both the Old and the New Testament, as symbols of the catechumen's progress (Jesus in the river Jordan represents Baptism), of salvation (Noah in the Ark), of healing (the paralytic and the bleeding woman) and of resurrection (Jonah, Lazarus). These scenes, like pagan paintings of the same period, are framed in narrow red and green lines. In the fourth century, with freedom granted to the Christian religion, the decoration in the catacombs shows a triumphant Church, with Christ victorious, seated among the twelve Apostles.

Marcus Aurelius (161–180) Martyrdom of Justin in 165	Septimius Severus (193–211)	Decius (249–251) Persecution of Christians	Constantine Constantine (306–337) With the Edict of Milan of 313, Christianity is no longer considered unlawful
Dynasty (96–192)	**The Severi (193–235)**	**Diocletian and Constantine (284–337)**	
Antoninus Pius (138–161) Commodus (180–192) Victor I Bishop of Rome 189–192	Caracalla (211–217) Calixtus Bishop of Rome 217–222 Caracalla	Diocletian (284–305) Many measures against Christians	Constantius Chlorus (305–306) The year 306 marks the end of persecutions in the West

Catacombs of St Calixtus

PRACTICAL INFORMATION
Catacombs of St Calixtus
110 Via Appia Antica.
☎ 06 513 01 51/
06 51 30 15 80.
FAX 06 51 30 15 67.
🚌 218, 660.
Closed Wednesday;
month of February.

These catacombs are situated two to three miles down the Via Appia Antica, in a location already widely used for pagan burials, and form a very large system, made up of overground as well as underground cemeteries from the end of the second century. Originally separate, they were eventually joined together to create a single vast network of communal catacombs.

The Arch of Drusus and the Porta Appia, also called Porta di San Sebastiano, in an old engraving.

The Catacombs of St Calixtus. They are situated between the second and third mile down the Via Appia Antica, which the Romans called 'the queen of all roads' because of its age and importance. The road was named by the censor Appius Claudius the Blind, who had it built in 312 B.C., and along it there were numerous pagan funerary monuments, some still visible today.

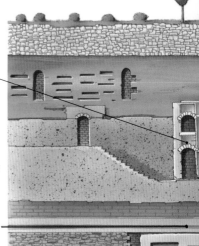

The first level, 6–7 metres from the surface.

The second level is more extensive, since it contained the venerated tombs, and the faithful wished to be buried next to them.

The third level, 25–26 metres deep.

The 'cubicula of the Sacraments', so called because of the paintings referring to the Eucharist and Baptism.

The crypt of Melchiades, dug in the fourth century, was dedicated to Pope St Melchiades (or Miltiades), who was Pope Eusebius' successor, and persuaded the Emperor Maxentius to restore to the Church all property confiscated in 303.

The tomb of Cornelius, with one of the beautiful inscriptions in verse by Pope Damasus.

The catacombs were lit by oil lamps.

The crypt of St Cecilia, next to the crypt of the Popes, held the body of the martyr St Cecilia, an object of devotion in the early Middle Ages.

131

Painting of a banquet in one of the cubicula of the Sacraments.

At the beginning of the third century the cemetery was the property of the Christian community, and was regarded as the principal cemetery of the Church of Rome. Pope Zephyrinus (199–217) entrusted its management to his principal deacon, Calixtus, after whom it was named. By the end of the early Middle Ages, the catacombs had been forgotten, and were rediscovered by the archaeologist Giovanni Battista de Rossi, who began his excavations there in 1849.

St Calixtus became Pope in 217, was martyred in 222, and was buried in the cemetery of Calepodius on the Via Aurelia. Famous martyrs such as St Tarsicius and St Cecilia were buried in the catacombs of St Calixtus, as well as most of the third-century Popes.

The burial complex consists of an area above the surface, and the catacombs proper underground. There were many buildings at ground level: funerary enclosures, pagan and Christian mausoleums, and a basilica, now lost, dedicated to St Cornelius by Pope St Leo the Great. The eastern and western *tricore* (funerary buildings with apses on three sides) survive. In the floor of the western *tricora* a multiple burial was discovered, later identified as the tomb of Pope Zephyrinus, Calixtus' predecessor, and of St Tarsicius. The eastern *tricora*, originally the mausoleum of a wealthy Christian, contains a collection of sarcophagi and, as of 1994, the tomb of Giovanni Battista de Rossi. The first zone is one of the oldest

POPES BURIED IN ST CALIXTUS

190–228	229–258	259–288	289–314
Anteros (235–236)	Stephen (254–257)		Melchiades (311–314)
Zephyrinus (199–217)	Cornelius (251–253)	Caius (283–296)	
Pontianus (230–235)	Fabian (236–250)	Sixtus II (257–258)	
	Lucius (253–254)	Eusebius (309–310)	

areas, and contains the crypts of the Popes and St Cecilia. Originally, two parallel galleries were created, each served by a stair. Later excavation created a grid of galleries on a rectangular plan. Opening onto one of the galleries are the 'cubicula of the Sacraments', so-called because of painted scenes referring to Baptism and the Eucharist, which date from the early third century, and are among the earliest examples of Christian painting. The crypt where almost all the Popes of the third century were buried is in this area, and nearby is the crypt of St Cecilia, an object of devotion in the early Middle Ages.

The crypt of the Popes owes its present appearance to Pope Damasus (366–384), who carved two remarkable inscriptions there.

The crypts of Lucina and the tomb of Pope St Cornelius (251–253), who died in exile in Civitavecchia and was buried in an underground chamber next to the Via Appia Antica, are also very ancient. It was originally separate from the cemetery administered by Calixtus, but the Roman matron Lucina, who owned it, later allowed the Christian community to use it. This is where the tomb of Cornelius, embellished by Pope Damasus, is found, with its Byzantine paintings of Cornelius and his close friend St Cyprian, Bishop of Carthage. Here are also the crypts named after Lucina, decorated with very early paintings.

A third, also originally separate, zone is that of Pope St Eusebius (309). Its crypt has the inscription by Pope Damasus mentioning the interesting question of the *lapsi* (those who denied their faith when facing martyrdom). In front of it is the spacious double *cubiculum* of Pope St Caius (283–296), and, nearby, the *cubiculum* of the martyrs, possibly from the time of Diocletian, Calocerus and Parthenius.

The galleries, with cells opening on both sides.

Catacombs of St Sebastian

PRACTICAL INFORMATION
Catacombs
of St Sebastian
136 Via Appia Antica.
📞 06 785 03 50.
FAX 06 784 37 45. 🚌 660.
Closed Sundays and
mid-November–
mid-December.

This cemetery, originally called *ad catacumbas* (next to the area of subsidence) because of the pozzolana earth extracted there and used for cement in local building, was in time given the name of St Sebastian, the martyr who is buried there. The burial ground remained accessible throughout the centuries, and the term 'catacombs' has been extended to refer to all underground Christian cemeteries.

Another name for the same complex is *memoria apostolorum*, meaning 'memory of the Apostles', because for a certain period of time Peter and Paul were venerated there. The area has been intensively used since the first century A.D., and built upon in various ways throughout different historical periods.

The basilica was built in 1608 at the behest of Cardinal Scipione Borghese, by completely reconstructing the existing fourth-century basilica, and making use of its central nave. Flaminio Ponzio was put in charge of the work and it was completed by Giovanni Vasanzio.

The poem by Pope Damasus for the martyr Eutychius, buried in the catacombs, is noteworthy; it is the only one of his inscriptions to survive complete. Also remarkable are the carved wooden ceiling; the altar with the urn containing the remains of St Sebastian and the statue of the saint; the Chapel of the Relics, containing one of the arrows that pierced him; the column where he was tied up and the stone bearing the footprint believed to be Jesus' (as related in the *'Quo Vadis'* story); and the Albani Chapel, designed by Carlo Fontana, with decoration dedicated to the martyred Pope St Fabian (236–250).

The church of *Quo Vadis*, situated between the Via Appia and the Via Ardeatina, refers to a famous story of St Peter's captivity. Having been persuaded by zealous followers in the community to leave Rome and avoid martyrdom, Peter was on the point of leaving the city when, at the place where the present church stands, Christ appeared to him. The Apostle asked, in surprise: *'Domine, quo vadis?'* (Where are you going, Lord?). And the Lord replied: 'I am going to Rome to be crucified for the second time'. St Peter understood, and returned to Rome to face his martyrdom. The church contains a copy of the stone bearing the Lord's footprint (the original is in the basilica of San Sebastiano).

The original basilica was dedicated by Constantine to Peter and Paul. All that is left of it is the outer nave: the long spaces to the right and to the left of the present basilica. The former is used as a ticket office for the catacombs, and houses a rich collection of local sarcophagi. The latter is partly used as an exit from the catacombs, partly as church sacristy and partly as a museum of inscriptions with an interesting scale model of the various phases of construction. There were huge mausoleums adjacent to Constantine's basilica, among them the so-called 'Platonia', built in the fourth century by the Pannonians (from the middle Danube) living in Rome, in which the martyr Quirinus, Bishop of the Pannonian city of Siscia, was laid to rest.

The catacombs have always been open. Among those who spent hours there in prayer were St Bridget of Sweden and her daughter St Catherine, St Philip Neri (who included them in the pilgrimage of the Seven Churches), St Pius V and St Charles Borromeo. The crypt where St Sebastian is buried, with a bust of the saint attributed to Bernini, and the *cubiculum* of St Philip Neri are both worth visiting.

The Martyrdom of St Sebastian, *by Andrea Mantegna.*

The crypt of St Sebastian *was linked to the church by two staircases, still visible today.*

The small villa is decorated with frescoes framed by narrow red and green lines (first decades of the third century). It was probably the seat of a funerary committee, whose job it was to ensure that its members received proper burial.

The model shows the unique structure of the fourth-century basilica, with its elliptical plan, like that of Roman circuses. Constantine ordered many basilicas be built in this style near important sanctuaries in the outskirts of Rome.

The *triclia* is a space enclosed by a portico, originally open, where Christians would venerate Peter and Paul or their relics. The hundreds of scratched supplications addressed to the two Apostles testify to the ritual banquets that took place in their memory. The reason why this devotion took place on the Via Appia was probably because the martyrs could not be venerated at their respective tombs in the Vatican and on the Via Ostiensis, because of the violent persecution of Christians by the Emperor Valerian in the second half of the third century. Constantine later had the basilica built on the site.

Below the *triclia* was a piece of land with three mausoleums (of Clodius Hermes, of the Innocentiores, and of the Ascia), magnificent pagan structures with painted and stucco decorations. Inscriptions and paintings of New Testament subjects confirm that, from the third century, Christians were also buried there. To the west of the mausoleums are the large and small villas, both dating from pagan times.

The oldest and deepest area (12 metres below the basilica) reveals pagan *columbaria* (chambers with many wall niches to hold the urns containing the ashes), and poor burials in the pozzolana quarry.

Catacombs of Domitilla

The catacombs of Domitilla extend along the old Via Ardeatina.

They grew out of clusters of underground burial chambers, some of them belonging to pagan families who then joined the Christian community. As the number of burials increased, the catacombs joined up, forming a single huge network, with over 12 kilometres of galleries. They are the largest in Rome, and Antonio Bosio almost lost his way in them.

The most important martyrs venerated here are two soldiers, Nereus and Achilleus, perhaps praetorian guards, who were probably victims of the terrible persecutions of Diocletian.

Another martyr mentioned in the sources, but whose true history is a matter of debate, is Petronilla. She is the subject of an entirely uncorroborated story that she was St Peter's daughter, perhaps because of the similarity of their names.

Petronilla was known as the 'succour of the Frankish nation', and for that reason her remains were moved to the chapel of the Frankish Kings in the Vatican (later destroyed to make way for the present St Peter's basilica) during the time of Paul I (757–767).

In the early Middle Ages, the cemetery fell into a state of serious neglect and was unsafe, as Pope Gregory the Great himself lamented in a memorable sermon.

For that reason, the cult of the two martyrs gradually moved to the very ancient parish church near the Baths of Caracalla (the fourth-century 'parish church of Fasciola').

The catacombs are arranged on two levels. Given their size, it is not possible to visit the whole cemetery, but only to follow a set route through part of it. Starting at the entrance, we come to:

PRACTICAL INFORMATION
Catacombs of Domitilla
282 Via delle Sette Chiese.
[06 511 03 42/
06 513 39 56.
FAX 06 513 54 61.
▦ 218, 714.
Closed Tuesday;
month of January.

*The **cubiculum, or burial chamber, of Diogenes the digger** is a fourth-century crypt, perhaps occupied by the leader of the workmen who excavated the cata-combs. Damage caused in the eighteenth century by efforts to remove the frescoes can be seen in the picture.*

The underground chamber of the Flavii. *Flavia Domitilla, before her exile, had put at the disposal of the Christian community her properties on the Via Ardeatina, thought to be where the catacombs were located.*

(1) The basilica of Sts Nereus and Achilleus. The present building dates from the end of the fourth century, in the papacy of Siricius (384–399), who continued his predecessor Damasus' veneration of the martyrs.

It was built on top of a private burial chamber in which the two martyrs had been laid. Petronilla must also have been buried near them. The building, which is half underground, is of considerable grandeur. It was abandoned in the ninth century, and rediscovered following excavations by de Rossi in 1874. A narthex stands in front of the body of the church, which has an apse. The interior is divided into three naves by columns whose capitals have been taken from elsewhere. The upper part of the church and the roof were reconstructed after it was discovered. The burial place of Nereus and Achilleus corresponded to the present altar. Remains of the early medieval *schola cantorum*, or choir school, can be seen. In the church is a collection of sarcophagi and inscriptions excavated in the surrounding area.

(2) Near the basilica can be seen a *cubiculum* with a noteworthy late-fourth-century painting

The basilica of Sts Nereus and Achilleus.
They are the two martyrs most venerated in the catacombs of Domitilla. An inscription of Pope Damasus describes them as two soldiers who converted to Christianity. In order to place the altar near their tombs, several galleries had to be destroyed.

of St Petronilla, leading the deceased Veneranda into Paradise.

(3) One of the oldest clusters is the burial chamber of the Flavii, initiated at the end of the second century for private pagan burials, with large niches for sarcophagi and fine naturalistic painting. During the third century, Christians were buried there, and decoration inspired by Scripture was added. De Rossi believed that members of the family of the Flavii, Christian members of the nobility and relatives of Domitilla, may have been buried there, but there is no evidence for this. The external façade of the chamber, a well and an area for the ritual of the funeral feast, as well as seats for banquets, all survive. The *cubiculum* of Cupid and Psyche, elegantly painted, completes the complex.

(4) The so-called 'great stair' area of Tor Marancia is very ancient, and was deepened several times. Of note are the *cubiculum* of the Good Shepherd, with paintings from the mid-third century, and the *cubiculum* of David.

(5) Another ancient and once separate burial is called the *cubiculum* of Ampliatus, from its owner's name, carved on a large marble tablet.

Of particular interest are the loftier, arched tombs of the Minor Apostles, the *cubiculum* of Diogenes the digger (noteworthy because its frescoes show the tools used by the workmen who excavated the catacombs), the *cubiculum* of Orpheus, the Crypt of the Six Saints and the Crypt of the Bakers, the painting of the Madonna with four Magi and the arched tomb with a mosaic of Christ between Peter and Paul.

Christ between Peter and Paul, *in one of the very few mosaics preserved in the catacombs.*

Flavia Domitilla.
The catacombs of Domitilla bear the name of a noble-woman, niece of Flavius Clemens, Consul in A.D. 95, who had married a niece of Domitian's (he was Emperor from 81 to 96), also called Flavia Domitilla. This branch of the Flavian clan seems to have had Christian sympathies, because pagan historians speak of punishments inflicted for religious reasons on the Consul and his wife: he was sentenced to death, and she was exiled to the island of Ventotene. But the Christian historian Eusebius tells us that Flavia Domitilla, the Consul's niece, was sentenced by Domitian to be deported to the island of Ponza with other Roman matrons, because she was a Christian.

Catacombs of Priscilla

PRACTICAL INFORMATION

Catacombs of Priscilla
430 Via Salaria.
【 FAX 06 86 20 62 72.
🚌 319.
Closed Monday;
month of January.

Priscilla must have been the founder of the cemetery, or else the donor of the land on which it was built.

As a surviving funerary inscription shows, Priscilla was related to the aristocratic family of the Acilii, mentioned by the historians Suetonius and Dio Cassius, who record that a certain Acilius Glabrio, Consul in A.D. 91, was sentenced to death by Domitian, with members of other senatorial families, probably for following the Christian faith.

These historical sources locate the burial places of many martyrs and Popes in Priscilla's catacombs. Among the most famous recorded are the brothers Felix and Philip, sons of St Felicitas, martyred in 304 in the Diocletianic persecutions, with their five other brothers: Alexander, Martial, Vitalis, Sylvanus and Januarius. Among Popes, they mention Marcellinus (296–304), Marcellus (308–309), Sylvester (314–335), Liberius (352–366), Siricius (384–399), Celestine (422–432) and Vigilius (537–555). This makes it the third most important papal cemetery, after the Vatican Grottos and the catacombs of St Calixtus.

The cryptoporticus
was used as a burial place by a patrician family, and later joined to the catacombs. It houses the very precious Greek Chapel.

The galleries of the Arenario, originally excavated in order to extract a type of earth called pozzolana, were used as burial places by the Christians.

The catacombs, situated on the ancient Via Salaria Nova (so called because it was used to bring salt to Rome from the Adriatic), are one of the largest. They are constructed on two levels, the upper, and older, being irregular and unplanned, while the lower is very orderly, with large parallel galleries, branching at right angles. The upper level can be visited, and contains:

Madonna and Child with the prophet Balaam, the earliest representation of the Mother of God in the Western world. It dates from 230–240.

(1) The *cubiculum* of the Veiled Woman, with paintings of the second half of the third century, representing salient moments from the life of a young woman, clearly the one buried in the *cubiculum*: marriage, motherhood and death.

(2) The niche of the Madonna and Child with the prophet Balaam, indicated by a star (see Numbers 24:17). The tenderness with which Mary is depicted holding the child close to her is particularly worth noting. Some people believe it is not Balaam but another prophet (Isaiah, Micah or David) who is represented, on the basis of other relevant biblical references.

(3) The central area of the Arenario consists of a series of galleries originally dug out in order to extract the typical Roman pozzolana earth, used

A view of the Greek Chapel, recently restored. In the foreground is the cycle of frescoes of Susanna.

**Women in the early
Christian community.**
Women played a very
important role in the earliest Christian community,
because it was the
generosity of noblewomen
that gave the Church
human and material
resources to meet the
needs of the poor and the
community. We know the
names of some of these
generous benefactresses,
including Prisca, Lucina,
Priscilla, Domitilla,
Commodilla, Generosa
and Octavilla. They
provided houses and land
that the community could
use to build churches and
cemeteries. But at the
same time, many of them,
in Africa, Spain, Sicily and
Asia Minor, as well as
Rome, paid by martyr-
dom for professing
the new faith.
Among the most
famous Roman
women martyrs
are St Agnes,
St Emerentiana,
St Cecilia, St
Felicitas (who
gave her life
with her seven
sons, Sylvanus,
Vitalis, Martial,
Alexander,
Felix, Philip and
Januarius), St Bassilla,
St Beatrice, St
Eugenia, St Thecla
and St Petronilla.

St Cecilia,
by Parmigianino.

to make the best quality building cement. About the first quarter of the third century, the Christian community re-used these galleries as a burial place for poor people, saving labour since they had already been excavated. The simple inscriptions in red lead on the slabs that close the burial recesses are of interest.

(4) The cryptoporticus and Greek Chapel. This is an underground space, with masonry walls, originally the burial place of a high-ranking family, and only later linked to the catacombs. The Greek Chapel, so called because it contains Greek inscriptions, is important for its late third-century frescoes. They show unusual scenes, including a cycle of the trial of Susanna, a eucharistic banquet and the phoenix in the flames, a pagan emblem adopted by the Christians; there was an ancient belief that this bird could rise from its own ashes.

(5) The burial place of the Acilii. This was originally a large water tank belonging to a cemetery at ground level, and was later used for Christian burials. Inscriptions of the noble Acilii family, relatives of Priscilla, were found here.

(6) The basilica of Pope St Sylvester is outside the catacombs, in the present Villa Ada. At the beginning of the fourth century, Pope Sylvester had a basilica built in the cemetery above the ground, whose altar was in the same position as the tomb of the martyrs Felix and Philip. Sylvester himself and Pope Siriacus were buried there.

Catacombs of St Agnes

These catacombs take their name from Agnes, the celebrated Roman martyr, who was buried there and who, we can be fairly sure, was a victim of the bloody persecutions of Diocletian. Many authors in antiquity, including Ambrose, Damasus and Prudentius, were fascinated by this heroic young girl, and wrote about her. It is, however, debatable whether Ambrose wrote the well-known hymn about her.

These texts tell us that Agnes was only twelve when she died, but there is great uncertainty about how she was put to death. Damasus speaks of her being burned at the stake, Ambrose and Prudentius of beheading, while the hymn says that the veins of her neck were cut. Prudentius refers to a detail of the torture Agnes endured, which would be frequently exploited in later legendary stories about the saint: she was exposed naked in a brothel, in a vault of the stadium of Domitian, on the site of the present Piazza Navona. In the early Middle Ages there was in fact a small chapel there, dedicated to her, later replaced by the large seventeenth-century church of Francesco Borromini, Sant' Agnese in Agone.

The young martyr's body was then laid in a burial chamber belonging to her family, on the left of the Via Nomentana, at the present-day Porta Pia. The cemetery, which became a communal one, was soon named after her.

From the beginning, Agnes's tender age and extraordinary strength of mind inspired deep devotion among both Romans and foreigners. She was greatly venerated, even by the family of the Emperor Constantine. In fact, on this site was built one of the typical elliptical churches of the Constantinian period, with an extraordinary round mausoleum, known as the Mausoleum of Santa Costanza, where the Emperor's daughter Constantia was buried. In the time of Pope

PRACTICAL INFORMATION
Catacombs of St Agnes
349 Via Nomentana.
☎ 06 86 20 54 56
FAX 06 861 08 40.
🚌 36, 36, 37, 60, 136, 137.
Opening hours 9 a.m.–12 p.m., 4–6 p.m.
Closed Sunday (and holidays) in the morning, Monday afternoon.

St Agnes, *martyred at the age of twelve, was greatly venerated by both Romans and foreigners, from the time of her death. Photograph: St Agnes praying, detail of marble slab.*

The Mausoleum of Santa Costanza *was built in the fourth century on a circular plan. The dome and drum are supported by arches resting on twelve pairs of granite columns.*

Symmachus (498–514) a small basilica was built, directly above Agnes's tomb. Pope Honorius (625–638) built on the burial site the present monumental, half-underground basilica of Sant'Agnese.

A tour of this sanctuary is fairly complicated but of great interest, because of the number and importance of archaeological finds.

Going underground from the outside, we see:

The elliptical Constantinian basilica: unfortunately these buildings proved not to be very durable, since they were all destroyed or only partially survive, except for the above-mentioned San Sebastiano.

Only the walls of the basilica, including the curve of the apse, remain, pierced by windows. It was built through the good offices, and at the expense, of Constantina or Constantia, daughter of the Emperor Constantine, who had converted to Christianity and whom later legends turned into a saint; hence the name Santa Costanza.

Catacombs of Sts Marcellinus and Peter

Situated on the old Via Labicana, now the Via Casilina, near the modern church of that name, these were built in what was the heart of the great Imperial property *ad duas lauros* ('at the two laurels'), which extended from the Porta Maggiore, in the Aurelian Walls, as far as Rome's most easterly suburb. In the late second century A.D., before the Christian cemetery existed, this was the burial ground of the *Equites singulares Augusti*, the Emperor's horse guards, a select body many of whose grave-stones have been found, re-used as building material; from the middle of the third century, Christians began to excavate galleries beneath it, to bury their dead. As in the other great catacombs, they first dug separate clusters of burial chambers which gradually expanded to form a vast cemetery, used by residents of one of the most densely populated parts of Rome, Subura. When the tombs of a number of martyrs were placed there, it brought a great expansion of the cemetery. They included Peter the exorcist and Marcellinus, a priest, both victims of Diocletian, buried in a crypt in the catacombs, Tiburtius, whose mausoleum is above ground, Gorgonius, buried in the catacombs, but whose tomb has not been identified, and the Crowned Martyrs, saints from Pannonia who were venerated, perhaps in the form of relics, in a crypt in the cemetery, before being transferred to the church of Santi Quattro Coronati in the city.

After his victory at the Milvian Bridge in 312, the Emperor Constantine completely transformed the site. He destroyed the cemetery of the *Equites singulares* and added notable buildings to the sanctuary, including a large elliptical basilica, a circular mausoleum and two enclosures at the sides of the basilica, containing many private mausoleums. Of all Constantine's construction, only the ruins of the domed

PRACTICAL INFORMATION
Catacombs of Sts Marcellinus and Peter
461 Via Casilina.
⊞ 105.
🚇 Roma Laziali.

Fresco in the catacombs, from the turn of the fifth century, showing Christ between St Peter and St Paul, and below, the principal martyrs venerated ad duas lauros: St Peter, St Marcellinus, St Tiburtius and St Gorgonius.

The Chapel of Sts
Marcellinus and Peter, which
led to the catacombs, was
built at the behest of Urban
VIII (Barberini) in 1638.

Funeral banquet,
part of the rite of the refrigerium, *in the catacombs
of Sts Marcellinus and Peter.*

mausoleum remain. They were originally covered in rich marble and mosaic, in the same style
as those in Santa Costanza. In a niche in the
mausoleum there was a magnificent red porphyry sarcophagus, now in the Vatican
Museums, containing the remains of Augusta
Helena, the Emperor's mother. In the seventeenth century, a small church with a presbytery
was built inside the mausoleum; there are plans
to turn it into a museum for the site.

Following Constantine's building projects,
the cemetery became one of the most notable in
the outlying parts of Rome.

Pope Damasus also lavished attention on it,
embellishing the venerated tombs and giving
them his distinctive verse inscriptions. The catacombs boast an exceptional wealth of paintings,
with frescoes in over 85 rooms showing fresh
and lively scenes of both pagan and Christian
inspiration. Among them should be mentioned
the pictures of the diggers, the workers who
excavated the cemetery, and the banqueting
scenes. They probably show family gatherings
connected with the very ancient ritual of the *refrigerium*, performed in memory of a deceased
relative on the anniversary of the day of his or
her death.

 ON DILEXERUNT ANIMAS SUAS
USQUE AD MORTEM (Revelation 12:11)

Giving life for Christ

Spiritual Message

How strange: a place representing death is the greatest sign of life. This is the meaning of visiting the catacombs: touching the roots of Christianity so as to discover the faith of those who have 'loved not their lives unto death' (Revelation 12:11). Sebastian, Nereus and Achilleus, Priscilla, Agnes . . . Men and women like so many others, yet they carry within them an un-conquerable conviction: Christ is humanity's freedom.

Entering the catacombs, one is confronted by the half-hearted way faith is lived by so many Christians. The martyrs of the Church belonging to the first millennium, like those of our time, give witness to a convincing belief: a life which is authentically Christian is the only way to experience the joy of being sons and daughters of God. This is also the message of many of our brothers and sisters in our time, living witnesses to a life which is faithful to Christ and to their neighbour. The life which is not ready to enter into any compromise is that of the martyrs as a result of wars, religious persecutions, in search of justice and solidarity.

The catacombs are a reminder for every pilgrim. They recall a very important memory. Getting to know those who witnessed a coherence in living God's call means understanding that the martyr reflects the face of the Church. Secondly, it is an invitation to become bearers of the Gospel message. With con-viction and courage, each one of us can give witness to the hope within to anybody who asks the reason why. 'The believer who has seriously pondered his Christian vocation, including what Revelation has to say about the possibility of martyrdom, cannot exclude it from his own life's horizon' (IM, 13).

VI

THE BASILICAS
OF SANTA PUDENZIANA
AND SAN CLEMENTE

ONSURREXISTIS
CUM CHRISTO (Colossians 3:1)

Risen with Christ

Spiritual Introduction

Christianity is a fact, an event: the death and resurrection of Christ. We may accept or reject a fact. To accept it is to enter in joy, because 'joy is the sentiment of reality' (Simone Weil). The stronger the perception of reality, the greater is the joy. The reality of the faith opens horizons of endless cheerfulness. Not only for the future, but also for the present, for every ordinary day. They mark the days and the hours, they colour our feelings, they bring peace.

Christians belong to resurrection, at least potentially. They 'have been raised up to be with Christ' (Col 3:1). This is where joy comes from. It is up to them to take possession of the gift and have full access to it. 'Christ has preceded us. We, too, have already been raised up, although only in hope' (St Augustine).

'Christian joy is the spiritual sharing in the unfathomable joy, both divine and human, which is in the heart of Jesus Christ glorified... All those who believe in Christ are called to share in this joy (John 17:13)' (GD, 2, 3). Joy is a fruit of the Spirit (Gal 5:22). It animates faith (2 Cor 1:24), it nourishes hope (Rom 15:13), it is expressed by

The Resurrection, by Piero della Francesca,
Civic Museum, Sansepolcro (Arezzo)

*charity, it is associated with prayer and thanksgiving
(1 Thess 5:16) through the nearness of Christ (Phil
4:4–5), i.e., of his kingdom, which is joy (Rom 14:17).*

*The Gospel is the good news of salvation that is
transformed into the joy of communion of the human
person with Jesus Christ and the Father (1 John 1:3–4). It
therefore denotes the whole of life, it lies beneath its
unfolding, it is not lost even in the hour of suffering,
when it becomes acceptance and surrender.*

*A sad Christian is a contradiction. He could be
afflicted, suffering, crucified – resurrection comes after
the cross – but never desperate. He knows that he has
been chosen for a plan of love, that he is loved
personally. He is open to a joyful destiny, not only in the
eschatological sense, but one which he may enjoy
immediately, in the places he usually frequents.*

SANTA PUDENZIANA

PPARUIT PRIMO
MARIAE MAGDALENAE (Matthew 28:1)

He appeared first to Mary of Magdala

Reflection

Ancient pilgrim guides of the seventh century mention St Pudentiana, virgin and martyr, together with her sister Praxedes, both venerated in the cemetery of Priscilla. The Acts of the two saints, later than the sixth century, are not historically reliable. However, literary sources and monuments, combining tradition and legend, maintain that Pudentiana, a young girl from a rich family, was a member of the Christian community in Rome at the time of Bishop Pius (c.140–155).

Pudentiana testifies to the presence of consecrated young people in the Roman Church. At the end of the first century, there are already traces of a Church organization of young women. Up to the first half of the third century, they lived with their own families. Their life in the service of the community was such that St Cyprian considered them 'the most illustrious part of the Church of Christ'. St Pudentiana evokes the dignity the Church has always acknowledged in women, in spite of the historical influence that has often marginalized them and subjected them to 'aggressive male behaviour'. Like many witnesses of Christ in all ages, Pudentiana showed that 'feminine grace, gifts and characteristics have a lot to offer to the mission and the work of the Church because in the charismatic sense of the word, women lead it just like men and maybe even more'. (Pope John Paul II, Letter to Women, 3, 5).

Christ Enthroned in Glory, mosaic in the apse, Santa Pudenziana, Rome

Like all women who made the mystery of womanhood blossom in the Church and in humanity, which owes them 'a debt which can never be repaid', this distant sister of ours is a reminder of 'a universal recognition of the dignity of women... (If) there is present in the womanhood of a woman who believes ... a kind of inherent prophecy' and if the contribution of women is indispensable for the fullness and the harmony of the life of the Church (ibid., 3, 5-11), the 'feminine genius' is precious for the progress of humanity. In every sector of human activity, cultural, social, political and economic, women must always contribute, and society must fight the discrimination they still brutally suffer in many countries. To contribute to the liberation of women, it is enough for the Church to pay unceasing and unflagging attention to the attitude of Jesus to women, the first witnesses and heralds of the resurrection (Mark 16:9; Matt 28:8).

History, Art and Architecture

PRACTICAL INFORMATION
160 Via Urbana.
[C] 06 481 46 22.
[BUS] 16, 70, 71, 714.
[M] Cavour.
Opening hours 8 a.m.–
12 p.m., 3 p.m.–6 p.m.

Between the Esquiline and Viminal hills, lower down than the present level of Via Urbana and near Santa Maria Maggiore, is the basilica of Santa Pudenziana, dedicated, according to late hagiographic tradition, to one of two daughters of the senator Pudens.

It was a *titulus* or, as we would say today, parish church, built above a second-century Roman house with heated baths, which some believe was a place of worship (*domus ecclesiae*) before the time of Constantine, but without conclusive evidence.

Built at the end of the fourth or the beginning of the fifth century, in three naves with six columns on each side, the church was extensively altered, particularly at the turn of the sixteenth century by Francesco da Volterra. It now had a single nave, covered by a dome in

Frieze on the architrave of the portico

Mosaic in the apse *(detail), the earliest surviving example from a place of worship.*

The entrance doorway *is supported on two columns. The frieze on the architrave formed part of the eleventh-century door.*

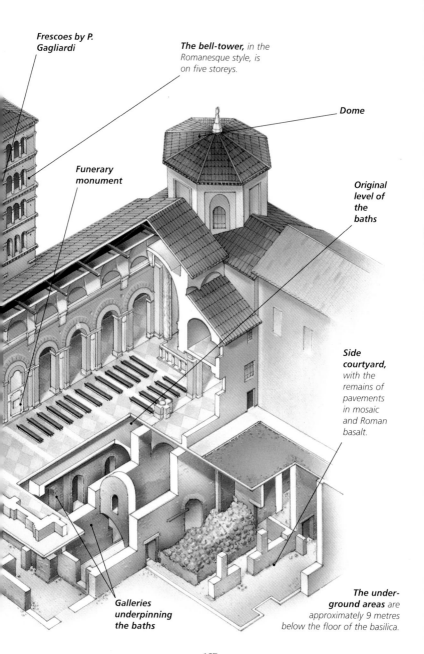

Frescoes by P. Gagliardi

The bell-tower, in the Romanesque style, is on five storeys.

Dome

Funerary monument

Original level of the baths

Side courtyard, with the remains of pavements in mosaic and Roman basalt.

Galleries underpinning the baths

The underground areas are approximately 9 metres below the floor of the basilica.

The underground galleries *below the level of the baths are 16 metres long, 4 metres wide and 7 metres high.*

The Chapel of St Peter *dates from 1595. It was built to commemorate the hospitality that St Peter is said to have enjoyed in the house of the senator Pudens.*

the area of the sanctuary. The fine mosaic in the apse survives from the early period, though heavily restored and reconstructed, and is one of the earliest in existence.

It is a huge composition, still in the classical tradition, showing Christ enthroned and blessing, surrounded by the college of the Apostles and, probably, allegorical figures of the Churches of the Gentiles and the Hebrews (others think they represent St Pudentiana and St Praxedes), crowning Peter and Paul.

A jewelled cross, a symbol of triumph, stands out in the background, placed at the summit of a hill, Golgotha, as does the imposing architecture of the celestial Jerusalem, with the symbols of the four Evangelists. The composition is framed in a background of soft clouds.

The mosaic presents the Lord Jesus as the centre and the joy of the Celestial Jerusalem. The Church of Christ, which marches joyfully towards Jerusalem, is represented by the house of Pudentiana, who gathers the assembly of the faithful. The scroll that Jesus holds in his left hand says that He, the Saviour, is their 'Preserver'. The right-hand side of the mosaic is largely a reconstruction of the original, while the lower section is lost. It showed the mystical Lamb and the dove of the Holy Spirit, and a mosaic inscription recording the names of the donors: Ilicius, Maximus and Leopardus.

The present Caetani Chapel is a radical transformation of an existing early Christian oratory, dedicated to St Pastor. The fine Romanesque bell-tower is from the early thirteenth century, and the doorway was made in the sixteenth century, using medieval materials.

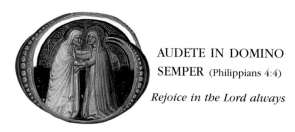

**AUDETE IN DOMINO
SEMPER** (Philippians 4:4)

Rejoice in the Lord always

Spiritual Message

Is it possible to experience joy in a situation where suffering and injustice seem to have the last word? The Gospel's answer is 'yes': 'Fear not; for, behold, I bring you good tidings of great joy, that shall be to all the people: for, this day, is born to you a Saviour, who is Christ the Lord, in the city of David' (Luke 2:10–11). The secret of joy lies in the presence of God within each person, knowing that one is loved by him and protected by his attentive love. All this even when the world around us seems to confirm the opposite. It is the same feeling that the disciples of Emmaus went through (Luke 24:13–35).

The Apostles, after the disappointment and the sorrow brought about by the death of Jesus Christ, experienced joy in meeting the risen Lord. Life suddenly changed. There were no more signs of death or defeat, but only life and freedom.

For this reason, the alternative between being with Christ or living away from him is reflected in the option of either living joyfully or going through an experience of sadness and absence of meaning.

Life can be lived in happiness and peace. All this is dependent on each one, in being able to accept God's love and be his disciple in the spirit of the Beatitudes. It remains true that the Christian message can give the impression of being strange or too idealistic.

But the witness of so many believers and saints who have lived this undeceiving hope proclaims to our time that to 'rejoice in the Lord always' (Philippians 4:4) is the key to happiness, especially when life is given freely. 'Presented in this way, deep joy has the tendency of being contagious, like life and love, of which it is a happy sign' (GD, IV).

SAN CLEMENTE

MOR ET MORS (Song of Songs 8:6)

Love as strong as death

Reflection

Clement of Rome, together with Ignatius of Antioch and Polycarp of Smyrna one of the Apostolic Fathers, i.e., those taught directly by the Apostles, is the third successor of Peter. He was Pope from 95 to 100. Irenaeus testified thus: 'Clement saw the blessed Apostles. He was in contact with them. He still had their preaching in his ears and their tradition before his eyes' (Adversus haereses, 3, 3, 3). When dissent broke out among the faithful in Corinth, Clement wrote them 'a very beautiful letter inviting them to re-establish peace, reanimating their faith and reaffirming the tradition of the Apostles, that was still fresh' (Irenaeus, ibid.). It is probably the oldest writing of the Christian tradition after the New Testament. It was defined as 'the epiphany of the Roman pontificate'.

In an atmosphere of nostalgia for the apostolic period, Clement, animated by a strong desire for purification, presented the organic structure of the Church as a body having many members, whose cohesive force lies in unity. Unity which can be endangered by envy, jealousy and ambition.

According to tradition, reflected in the Acts of the Martyrdom of St Clement *(fourth–sixth century), he was a martyr. His letter reveals a love as 'strong as death' (Song 8:6) for Christ and the Church, and a pastor's anxiety for its unity: 'Who can ever explain the bond of divine love?*

St Clement, mosaic in the apse,
San Clemente, Rome

Who can ever proclaim its greatness and beauty? The height to which it raises is ineffable. Love unites us to God, covers over many a sin (1 Peter 4:8), is always ready to excuse and to endure whatever comes. There is nothing vile or arrogant in love. Love does not instigate schism, does not rebel, always acts in all harmony … With love, the Lord drew us to himself, and out of the charity that he had for us, Jesus Christ our Lord, docile to the will of God, gave his blood' (St Clement, Letter to the Corinthians, *49).*

History, Art and Architecture

PRACTICAL INFORMATION
Via di San Giovanni in Laterano.
☎ 06 70 45 10 18.
🚌 81, 85, 87, 714.
Ⓜ Colosseo.
🚋 30b at Colosseo.
Open 9 a.m.–12.30 p.m.;
3.30–6.30 p.m. (6 p.m.
October–March) daily.
🚹 📷

The Apostles, *detail of the fresco below the mosaic in the apse.*

The flamboyant mosaic in the apse of the basilica of San Clemente, completed under Pope Paschal II in the first half of the twelfth century, has a complex symbolic significance, also connected with the large motif of acanthus branches, a reference to the Resurrection. The central theme is the Triumph of the Cross on whose arms, next to Christ, rest twelve doves representing the Apostles, between Mary and St John.

Acanthus scrolls grow naturally from the cross, framing a lively scene filled with small figures, both human and animal, while, lower down, two stags drink from the rivers of Paradise. The apsidal arch, in addition to the allegorical cities of Jerusalem and Bethlehem, depicts Christ with the symbols of the Evangelists, St Peter and St Clement, with the prophet Jeremiah, on one side, and St Lawrence, St Paul and the prophet Isaiah on the other. Underneath this, the early Christian motif of the Lamb of God appears again, surrounded by the twelve sheep, another symbol of the Apostles.

The church one enters today from Via San Giovanni in Laterano is the medieval one, with three naves ending in three apses, preceded by a four-sided portico; but the earlier phases of building at San Clemente can also be seen.

These are: the early Christian church, larger

CHRONOLOGY

Second century *Possibly a place of worship for Christians*	**867** *St Clement's remains are moved to Rome*	**1108** *New church built on the site of the fourth-century original*		**1857** *Father Mullooly discovers the original fourth-century church*
End of second century *Building of the temple of Mithras*				

A.D. 100	500		1000		1500		190

90–99 *Papacy of St Clement*	**Fourth century** *First church built in the courtyard of the existing Roman buildings*	**1084** *Church destroyed during the Norman invasion led by Robert Guiscard*	**1667** *Church and convent handed over to Irish Dominicans*	**1861** *Disco of th Rome ruin.*

162

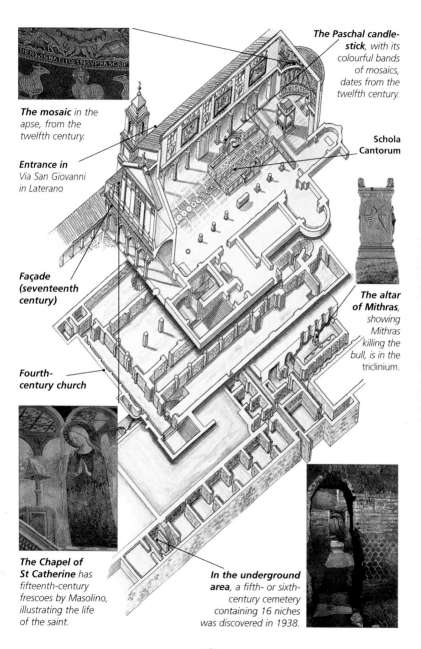

The Paschal candle-stick, *with its colourful bands of mosaics, dates from the twelfth century.*

The mosaic *in the apse, from the twelfth century.*

Schola Cantorum

Entrance in *Via San Giovanni in Laterano*

Façade (seventeenth century)

The altar of Mithras, *showing Mithras killing the bull, is in the triclinium.*

Fourth-century church

The Chapel of St Catherine *has fifteenth-century frescoes by Masolino, illustrating the life of the saint.*

In the underground area, *a fifth- or sixth-century cemetery containing 16 niches was discovered in 1938.*

The atrium with its four-sided portico, leading to the basilica.

The Schola Cantorum, (choir), dating from the sixth century, was preserved in the new church built in 1108.

than the later one, a Mithraic temple, and the remains of ancient Roman buildings.

All these building phases form a series of layers, which archaeological research carried out from the nineteenth century onwards has made coherent and accessible. Starting from the lowest level, the site was occupied by a public building dating from the first century A.D., and later by a set of domestic buildings, whose courtyard was turned into a place of worship by the followers of the Persian god Mithras.

The early Christian basilica was built in the fourth century. It enjoyed the status of parish church (*titulus*), had three naves and a narthex. The earlier structures are difficult to distinguish because of the massive foundations supporting the medieval church above.

Recent excavations have identified the baptistery attached to the early church.

Important frescoes have survived from the time of Pope Leo IV (847–855) and from the eleventh and twelfth centuries. They include the paintings of the *Legend of St Alexis* and the *Legend of Sisinnius*. Also greatly venerated is the tomb of St Cyril, who, with St Methodius, was one of those who took the Gospel to Eastern Europe. He devised the Cyrillic alphabet, still used in Russia. In the upper church, the Chapel of St Catherine contains a cycle of remarkable frescoes by Masolino da Panicale completed, perhaps in collaboration with Masaccio, between 1428 and 1431. Subjects depicted include the Crucifixion and episodes from the lives of St Ambrose and St Catherine of Alexandria.

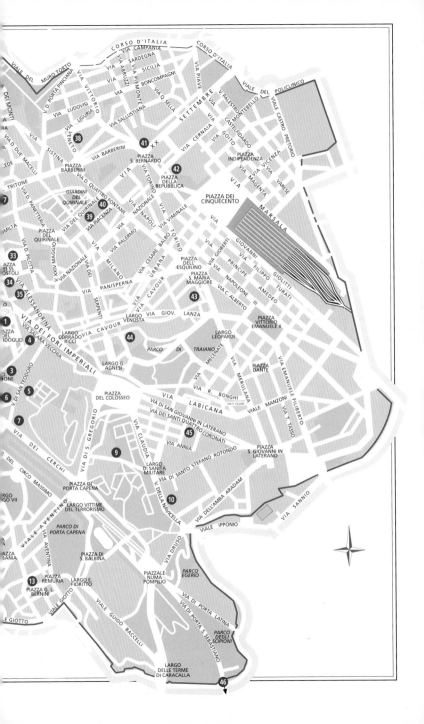

Historical Notes

SANTA MARIA IN ARACOELI ❶

4 Piazza del Campidoglio
Ⓜ *Colosseo*
🚌 *44, 56, 640, 715, 810*

The church was built, probably in the sixth century, on the northern side of the Capitol hill, on the site of the temple of Juno. It is preceded by a wide staircase of 124 steps, completed in 1348 under Cola di Rienzo. The name Aracoeli (altar of heaven) derives from a fourth-century legend that the Virgin appeared to Augustus. The present Franciscan church dates from the end of the thirteenth century. Changes to the interior carried out in the latter part of the sixteenth century meant that the apse with its frescoes by Pietro Cavallini had to be sacrificed. The present façade was built in the 1200s, but the three doors are later. The interior is divided into three naves by 22 columns salvaged from other buildings, and a wooden ceiling commemorating the battle of Lepanto (1571) with Mary and the Infant Jesus in the centre. The sanctuary contains a tenth- or eleventh-century icon of the Madonna and Child, venerated during the plague of 1348. In the left-hand transept, the Chapel of St Helena has a Cosmatesque altar and a twelfth-century figure of Mary appearing to the kneeling Augustus. In the Chapel of the Holy Child is a copy of the fifteenth-century statue in olive wood from the Garden of Gethsemane.

The fresco of the *Madonna and Child Enthroned between St Matthew and St John* is attributed to Pietro Cavallini.

SANTA MARIA IN CAMPITELLI ❷

9 Piazza Campitelli
Ⓜ *Colosseo, Circo Massimo*
🚌 *44, 56, 80, 640, 715, 810*

The church of Santa Maria in Campitelli, not far from Largo Argentina, contains a venerated image of Mary. It was rebuilt in the late Baroque style by Carlo Rainaldi in the first half of the seventeenth century. At the high altar is preserved the eleventh-century icon, made of silver leaf and enamel, called Santa Maria in Portico, *Romanus portus securitas*. It is believed to have saved Rome from an epidemic in 1656.

Santa Maria della Consolazione ❸

84 Piazza della Consolazione

Ⓜ Colosseo, Circo Massimo

🚌 44, 81, 95, 170, 628, 715, 810

In the old days the church of Santa Maria della Consolazione was attached to the hospital of the same name on the Vico Jugario on the slopes of the Capitol hill, built in 1470 and demolished in 1936. It was rebuilt by Martino Longhi the elder towards the end of the sixteenth century with three naves with side chapels, and it contains many valuable works with Mary as their theme. Above the high altar there is a venerated fresco depicting the *Virgin of Consolation*, dating from the Middle Ages, but reworked by Antoniazzo Romano at the end of the fifteenth century. Beside it are the *Nativity* and the *Assumption*; in the chapel to the right of the sanctuary is a thirteenth-century icon of the Virgin and in the second chapel on the right a *Madonna and Child with Saints* by Livio Agresti (1575). Also noteworthy, in another chapel, are the frescoes of the *Passion* by Taddeo Zuccari (1556).

Santi Cosma e Damiano ❹

1 Via dei Fori Imperiali

Ⓜ Colosseo, Circo Massimo

🚌 75, 85, 87, 117, 175, 186

This church was built by Felix IV (526–530) over pre-existing classical structures, identified as the library of the Forum of Peace, and a chamber belonging to the temple of the Divine Romulus, on the Via Sacra: the external wall had a cladding of 150 marble slabs, making up the ancient Forma Urbis, the monumental map of Rome at the time of the Severi. The church has remained largely unchanged since the first half of the seventeenth century, when the floor was raised by approximately 7 metres, because of water seepage, and the interior was altered by sacrificing the far ends of the mosaics in the original apse. Its dedication to the doctor-saints relates to the spread of their cult, especially during the sixth century. In the centre of the vault of the apse, Christ soars in heaven, dressed in gold, under the hand of God, and between Peter and Paul, who present Cosmas and Damian. Next come St Theodore and Pope Felix IV, the latter with a small model of the church in his hand; lower down is the Lamb of God with twelve sheep beside him, symbolizing the Apostles. The triumphal arch, possibly completed under Pope Sergius I (692–701), depicts the Apocalypse, with the mystic Lamb carrying the Cross.

San Teodoro

7 Via di San Teodoro
 Colosseo, Circo Massimo
44, 81, 95, 170, 715, 810

The earliest definitive evidence that a charitable institution consisting of a church and a convent existed on this site is from the ninth century. Until the sixteenth century, the bronze she-wolf from the Capitol was preserved here. The name comes from the legendary Roman soldier from Asia Minor, who was sent to the stake for refusing to offer up a sacrifice, and for burning down a temple dedicated to the goddess Cybele, probably under the Emperor Diocletian in the third century. His cult was widespread throughout the Greek and Latin Christian worlds. The church was nicknamed 'Santo Toto', and mothers would take their sick children there to be healed. Like the Mausoleum of Santa Costanza and Santo Stefano Rotondo, it is on a circular plan, and was restored under Nicholas V (1447–1455), as the recently excavated ancient ruins and the sixth-century mosaic show. Its present appearance departs from the design by Bernardo Rossellino; it was first renovated in 1643 on the orders of Cardinal Barberini, and later, in 1705, under Pope Clement XI, by the architect Carlo Fontana. In order to clear earth and water from the depression in the ground, Fontana designed the rectangular parvis in front of the church, accessible from street level by two curved converging staircases; he also added a chapel, the sacristy and a room for vestments. The church was handed over to the Society of the Sacred Heart of Jesus, also known as theConfraternita dei Sacconi Rossi, which promotes devotion to the Sacred Heart and fights blasphemy. It is also known for its special Good Friday ceremony. Inside there are two side altars and a high altar, the latter with an old Russian icon of the Virgin and Child. In the apse is a sixth-century mosaic depicting the Saviour between Sts Peter, Paul, Theodore and Cleonicus. The figure of St Theodore, cloaked in a gold-spangled mantle, was added at the time of the restoration carried out under Nicholas V.

San Giorgio in Velabro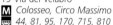

19 Via del Velabro
 Colosseo, Circo Massimo
44, 81, 95, 170, 715, 810

The church was built, probably by Popé Leo II (682–683), on a marshy piece of land called the Velabrum where, according to the legend, the shepherd Faustulus rescued Remus and Romulus. It is not far from the Arco degli Argentari, dating from the times of the Severi, and it was originally dedicated to St Sebastian. Pope Zacharias (741–752) ordered the relics of St George be moved there from the Lateran Palace.

The building was part of an ancient charitable institution established by the Church to assist the Christian community in Rome. The five-storey Romanesque bell-tower dates from the thirteenth century. The interior is divided into three irregular naves by salvaged columns with no bases. The fresco in the apse, depicting Christ, Mary and Sts George, Peter and Sebastian, is of the school of Cavallini, but heavily restored. In the raised sanctuary, the Cosmatesque altar is surmounted by a canopy with architrave, dating from the twelfth or thirteenth century. On 27 July 1993, the church's thirteenth-century portico, the gift of Prior Stefano Stella, and the convent were damaged by a bomb.

SANT'ANASTASIA ❼

Piazza di Sant'Anastasia
Ⓜ *Colosseo, Circo Massimo*
🚌 *81, 160, 628, 810*

A parish church (*titulus*) since the fourth century, and situated between the western edge of the Palatine hill and the Circus Maximus, it was later restored by various Popes: Damasus (366–384), Hilarius (461–468), John VII (706–707) and Gregory IV (827–844). Legend made

Anastasia, martyred during Diocletian's persecutions and venerated in Constantinople, where her relics had been transferred, a Roman martyr, and her name was superimposed on that of the woman who founded the *titulus Anastasiae* of the ancient basilica.

Between 1598 and 1618 Cardinal Sandoval had a new façade built in place of the earlier Renaissance one, but this was destroyed by a whirlwind in 1636.

The present façade, built of brick with two storeys of pilaster strips and twin bell-towers, was designed by L. Arrigucci for Urban VIII (1623–1644). In 1615 the altar of the Holy Cross was dedicated to the Confraternity of the Cross and St Anastasia, a guild of tailors and coat-makers. The interior was restored first in the early eighteenth century at the request of the Portuguese Cardinal Nuno da Cunha, and then again in the nineteenth century under Pius VII (1800–1823) and Pius IX (1846–1878). It is divided into three naves by six

pillars, with the marble columns salvaged from the early basilica placed against them. The coffered wooden ceiling dates from the eighteenth century, and the seventeenth-century Chapel of the Relics contains paintings by Lazzaro Baldi depicting episodes from the lives of St Charles Borromeo and St Philip Neri. In the area under the church are the ruins of a portico dating from the first century of the Empire and of a group of dwellings (*insulae*). Pope St Leo the Great, during the Mass at dawn on Christmas morning, gave a homily against Eutyches, the theologian who propounded the heresy that denied Christ's human nature: from then on, the Popes used to celebrate one of the three Christmas Masses at dawn at Sant'Anastasia.

SANTA MARIA IN COSMEDIN ❽

18 Piazza Bocca della Verità
Ⓜ *Colosseo, Circo Massimo*
🚌 *81, 160, 628, 810*

On the left-hand side of the portico of this church is the grotesque mask popularly known as the Bocca della Verità, or 'mouth of truth'. It is a Roman cap-stone, possibly from a well or a branch of the main sewer, the Cloaca Maxima, placed here in 1632, on top of a Corinthian capital. The first reports of the existence of a *diaconia*, a church with a charitable building attached to it, go back to the sixth century, and refer to Santa Maria *in Schola Graeca*, because the Byzantine-Greek community made it its main church. It was rebuilt in 782 by Pope

Adrian I, and sheltered those exiled under the iconoclastic persecutions of Constantine V Copronymus (774–780).

At that time it seems to have been called *Kosmidion* because of its rich decoration, though others say it referred to a building of that name in Constantinople. In the ninth century a sacristy and an oratory, dedicated to St Nicholas, were added. The complex was destroyed by Robert Guiscard in 1084, and restored by Pope Gelasius II (1118–1119). Later changes include a new façade on the portico, with a vestibule in the centre, under Calixtus II (1119–1124), and the Romanesque bell-tower of seven storeys. In the eighteenth century the church took on a Baroque

appearance, but was restored to its original style at the end of the nineteenth. It is divided into three naves, with pillars and salvaged columns, a pavement in imitation of the Cosmatesque style (the part in the Schola Cantorum is original), and a ceiling rebuilt in the late eighteenth century. The internal gallery, dating from the eighth century, but closed by Pope Calixtus II, was also renewed then. Roman structures, thought to belong to the residence of the Prefect in charge of food supplies, have been found under the church. The twelfth-century Schola Cantorum, with two pulpits and an iconostasis, and the red granite altar, with its late thirteenth-century canopy by Deodato, son of Cosma the younger, occupy much of the central nave. The crypt, in three sections, was carved out of an enormous block of tufa, possibly from the great altar of Hercules. Since 1639, a mosaic of the Adoration of the Magi, from the destroyed oratory of John VII (706–707) in St Peter's, has been displayed in the seventeenth-century sacristy, altered in the eighteenth century.

SANTI GIOVANNI E PAOLO

13 Piazza dei Santi Giovanni e Paolo
M *Circo Massimo*
🚌 *81, 175, 673, 810*

The church stands on the remains of the house of the two officials of Constantine's court martyred by Julian the Apostate for embracing the Christian faith and buried in their house in 361. The church was altered in the early eighteenth century, and at the end of the nineteenth, the remains of the saints' house were brought to light. The façade is divided into a portico, with eight columns, and an upper part with five arches supported on ancient marble columns. The Romanesque belltower, whose six upper storeys are decorated with ceramic discs in various colours, rests on a foundation of blocks of travertine marble, the remains of the temple of Claudius. The seven arches on the left, thirteenth- and fourteenth-century buttresses, rest on pieces of ancient Roman masonry. The interior, with three naves, contains a fresco by Pomarancio of 1588, *The Redeemer in Glory*, in the apse, and a porphyry basin at the high altar, with relics of the two saints. Underground are the remains of a pool, with second- and third-century frescoes, a pagan Roman house, an early Christian house (possibly that of the two saints) and an early medieval oratory. There is also a tiny room with ninth- and twelfth-century frescoes showing the martyrdom of the two saints.

SANTO STEFANO ROTONDO ⑩

7 Via di Santo Stefano Rotondo
M *Circo Massimo*
🚌 *81, 673, 810*

This church stands on the road running alongside the aqueduct of Nero, and dates from the time of Pope Simplicius I (468–483). Its mosaic and marble decoration was added between 523 and 530. It was the earliest church built in Rome on a circular plan, though its exterior was cruciform. It consisted of three concentric areas, with eight entrances and four radial chapels. The chapel of Sts Primus and Felician, with seventh-century decoration in the apse showing Christ between the two martyrs, survives.

SANTA SABINA ⓫

1 Piazza Pietro d'Illiria
Ⓜ *Circo Massimo*
🚌 *23, 44, 95, 170, 280, 716*

This early Christian basilica on the Aventine hill is practically intact, with its three naves and their columns, its broad windows, the mosaic with inscriptions in gold lettering on the inner façade and the allegorical figures of two women representing the Churches of the Jews and the Gentiles, the two main components of the Christian community headed by Peter and Paul. Building was started in the first half of the fifth century under Pope Celestine I (422–432) and completed under Sixtus III (432–440). The original decoration of the apse was replaced by a sixteenth-century fresco by Taddeo Zuccari, but

many of the panels of the wooden door, with the story of Moses and New Testament scenes, survive. They include the first appearance in Christian iconography of Christ crucified between the two thieves.

SANT'ALESSIO ALL'AVENTINO ⓬

23 Piazza Sant'Alessio
Ⓜ *Circo Massimo, Piramide*
🚌 *23, 280, 30, 75, 175, 715*

Dedicated in the third or fourth century to St Boniface the Martyr, it became a *diaconia* in the eighth, and was later also dedicated to St Alexis, by whose name it is known today. The medieval building from the time of Pope Honorius III (1216–1227) was altered in 1750 by order of Cardinal Querini. The Somaschi

order, present since 1846, initiated other restoration works. The bell-tower, the thirteenth-century crypt, and Cosmatesque work including the doorway, the floor and the small columns of the choir are all worth noting. In the right-hand arm of the transept is a thirteenth-century Byzantine icon of the Virgin.

SAN SABA ⓭

20 Piazza Bernini
Ⓜ *Circo Massimo, Piramide*
🚌 *95, 280, 175, 702, 719*

In 645 a group of monks from the monastery of Mar Saba, in Palestine, settled in a *domus* on the little hill where the church was later built. The antipope Constantine was held prisoner there in 768. The church first presents its vestibule, at the top of a flight of steps leading to a green courtyard overlooked by the façade. The original façade is hidden behind the portico and the fifteenth-century arcade. The interior consists of three naves divided by salvaged columns. The sanctuary is raised, with a crypt below it. Above its altar is a canopy supported on columns of black marble. There is a series of frescoes in the hemicircle

of the apse, painted for the Jubilee of 1575; it is a reproduction of an earlier mosaic. In the right-hand nave are preserved the remains of Cosmatesque work by Vassalletto. In the small nave on the left, originally perhaps a portico, are frescoes from the late eleventh or early twelfth century, depicting the Virgin, St Andrew, St Nicholas and St Sabbas. In the corridor leading to the sacristy are the remains of seventh- or eighth-century frescoes showing the monks of the Eastern community.

San Pietro in Montorio ⓮

2 Piazza San Pietro in Montorio
Ⓜ *Circo Massimo*
🚌 *44, 75, 710, 870, 871*

A chapel existed on this site at the end of the ninth century. In 1472 Sixtus V handed the church and convent over to the Spanish congregation of

the Amadeites and they, with the help of the King and Queen of Spain, began to build a new church, to a design by Baccio Pontelli and Meo del Caprino. It has a single nave, with frescoes by Sebastiano del Piombo (*The Flagellation, The Ascension* and *The Prophets,* dated 1518), by Pomarancio and Peruzzi in the second chapel, and by Vasari in the fourth. In 1503, Bramante was commissioned to build the famous 'Tempietto', to commemorate the martyrdom of St Peter. It is circular, consisting of a sanctuary surrounded by an ambulatory with 16 granite columns. An upper entablature and a small dome, whose drum is enlivened by alternating rectangular and curved niches, give San Pietro an air of harmony and

monumentality, in spite of its small size. In its classical form and perfect proportions it symbolizes the synthesis of ancient and Christian Rome.

San Crisogono ⓯

44 Piazza Sonnino
Ⓜ *Circo Massimo*
🚌 *44, 75, 710, 870, 871*

This is an old parish church (*titulus*), whose early Christian elements can be seen in the lower part, while the upper is a seventeenth-century transformation of the twelfth-century building. The original fifth-century church is parallel with it, but further to the left in relation to the medieval one. It has three naves, ending in a wide apse. The Confessio in the area of the sanctuary dates from the eighth century.

SANTA MARIA IN TRASTEVERE

14/c Via della Paglia
M *Circo Massimo*
🚌 *44, 75, 710, 870, 871*

This old parish church, built by Pope Julius I (337–352), retains the medieval appearance imposed on it by Pope Innocent II (1138–1148). The portico, which has a collection of pagan and early Christian inscriptions, and the façade were rebuilt in the eighteenth century. Outside, there is a thirteenth-century mosaic of the Virgin enthroned. In the centre of the wooden ceiling is Domenichino's *Assumption of the Blessed Virgin*, of 1617. In the centre of the apse, which dates from about the late twelfth century, is Christ crowning the Virgin Mary among saints and Popes. There are magnificent mosaic panels between the windows, made by Pietro Cavallini in 1291 and representing stories of the Virgin. Finally, the sixth- or seventh-century painting on the altar, in encaustic on wood, a technique typical of Roman painting, called the Madonna della Clemenza, is worth noting.

SANTA CECILIA

22 Piazza di Santa Cecilia
M *Circo Massimo*
🚌 *23, 44, 75, 280*

Recent excavation has identified significant features, including the fifth-century baptistery, which re-used a building with an apse from the time of Trajan, situated under the Chapel of the Relics. The remains also included parts of a house from the Imperial era, under the present church. A late account of St Cecilia's martyrdom says that was where she lived, and that the house was acquired by the Church, at her wish. Pope Paschal I (817–824) rebuilt the church and brought the martyr's remains from the catacombs of St Calixtus. The church today looks as it did in the eighteenth century, although works were carried out at various times, particularly at the turn of the thirteenth century (to the portico, the bell-tower, the right wing of the convent and the cloisters) and in the sixteenth century.

The church is flanked by the convent of the sisters and there is a broad medieval courtyard in front of it. It has three naves, divided by pillars, which, since the nineteenth century, enclose the 24 original Corinthian columns. The vault has paintings by Sebastiano Conca from about 1727,

showing the *Coronation of St Cecilia*. A corridor leading off the right-hand nave leads to the Chapel of the Bath, possibly the bath where the saint was martyred. It contains a tondo by Guido Reni depicting the *Marriage of St Cecilia and Valerian*, and above the altar a canvas by Reni of 1603, of the *Beheading* of the saint. In front of Arnolfo di Cambio's canopy of 1293 stands a statue of St Cecilia, of 1600, by Stefano Maderno. The mosaic in the apse, of about 820, is of high quality. It shows Christ blessing, crowned by the hand of God, and at his sides St Paul, St Cecilia and the Pope who paid for the church, carrying a model of it, and Sts Peter, Valerian and Agatha. Below, twelve lambs surrounding the Lamb of God are shown leaving the cities of Jerusalem and Bethlehem. In the nuns' choir is a late thirteenth-century fresco of the *Last Judgement* by Pietro Cavallini. Paintings of the *Annunciation*, *St Christopher, Jacob's Dream* and the *Deception of Isaac* all survive.

SANTA MARIA DEL POPOLO ⓲

12 Piazza del Popolo
Ⓜ *Flaminio*
🚌 *81, 628, 926*

In 1099 Pope Paschal II built a chapel in honour of the Virgin Mary above the Roman tombs of the Domitii family. The church was enlarged by Gregory IX, and rebuilt, perhaps by Andrea Bregno, between 1472 and 1478 by order of Sixtus IV, creating a museum with works by the greatest artists of the Renaissance and the seventeenth century. Bernini carried out extensive alterations to the façade and the interior. Worth noting are the chapels of the nobility: the Chigi Chapel (designed by Raphael with an altarpiece by Sebastiano del Piombo), the Della Rovere Chapel (with frescoes by Pinturicchio from 1485–1489), and the Cerasi Chapel, with two canvases by Caravaggio, the *Conversion of St Paul* and the *Crucifixion of St Peter* (1601–1602).

Behind the altar are the funerary monuments of Ascanio Sforza (1505) and Girolamo Basso Della Rovere (1507), by Andrea Sansovino. Above it are the two earliest stained glass windows in Rome, with stories of the Virgin and the childhood of Christ, made by the Frenchman Guillaume de Marcillat in 1509.

In the Cesi Chapel is the altarpiece of the *Assumption* by Annibale Carracci (1601). On the high altar of 1627 is a thirteenth-century painting, the Madonna del Popolo, traditionally said to have been painted by St Luke. In the apse are frescoes by Pinturicchio, showing the coronation of the Virgin, Evangelists, sibyls and Doctors of the Church. Bramante contributed to the transformation of the choir between 1500 and 1509.

TWIN CHURCHES OF THE PIAZZA DEL POPOLO ⑲

Santa Maria dei Miracoli:
528 Via del Corso
Santa Maria in Montesanto:
197 Via del Babuino
 Flaminio
🚌 *81, 628, 926*

In the Middle Ages, in what is now the Piazza del Popolo, a gate, the Porta San Valentino, opened in the Aurelian Walls, and from it ran the long, straight Via Lata (Via del Corso). At the beginning of the sixteenth century, Pope Leo X (Medici) (1513–1521) commissioned Raphael and Sangallo to create a road from the river port at Ripetta to Piazza del Popolo, the Via Leonina. A few years later, in 1523, the present Via del Babuino (Via Paolina) was started by Clement VII and completed by Paul III. It ran alongside the slope of the Pincian hill as far as Piazza di Spagna, creating one of the most important pieces of urban planning in Rome, the so-called 'Trident'. Before it was 'furnished' by Valadier, Sixtus V commissioned Domenico Fontana to install a large obelisk that had lain in the Circus Maximus. It is the oldest in Rome after the one at the Lateran, 36.50 metres high including its base. But it was Alexander VII (Chigi) who had the spectacular idea of building the twin churches at the head of the 'Trident'. It was a plan worthy of Rome's monumentality, and also one designed to attest to the city's sacredness. They were begun by Carlo Rainaldi and completed by Bernini and Carlo Fontana, and although they appear to be identical, in fact they are rather different. They each have a portico with a classical tympanum, evoking the solemnity of the Pantheon, and are covered by a large dome with fish-scale tiles. Each has a short bell-tower, providing a wonderful example of Baroque design, and creating a type of building on a central plan particularly well suited to an urban site that cannot be extended lengthways. The architectural elements produce an effect of grandeur designed to create a powerful impression of monumentality. On the right, towards Via Ripetta, is Santa Maria dei Miracoli, completed in 1597, which commemorates the miraculous image of the Virgin preserved at its high altar. It is circular, with two chapels on each side and an octagonal dome, and has sculptures by Antonio Raggi.

On the left, towards Via del Babuino, is Santa Maria in Montesanto, built on the site of an older church belonging to the Sicilian Carmelite order of Monte Santo. It was completed in 1675, on an elliptical plan with

180

three chapels on each side and a twelve-sided dome. It is celebrated for the 'Mass of the Artists', commemorating the Stations of the Cross, for which the models were made by great modern Italian sculptors.

SANTI AMBROGIO E CARLO AL CORSO ⑳

437 Via del Corso
 Spagna
🚌 32, 115, 913

Standing on the site of San Niccolò del Tufo, this church was rebuilt under the name of Sant'Ambrogio dei Lombardi, and in 1612 Onorio Longhi was given the task of enlarging it. It was then dedicated to St Ambrose and St Charles Borromeo. Longhi died, having only designed the project, a façade with two bell-towers, a large dome and four

smaller ones. His son, Martino Longhi the younger, took over, and in 1651 Pietro da Cortona created the apse, the dome and the high altar. The façade, crowned by a very high tympanum, was completed in 1684 by the two architect friars Gian Battista Menicucci and Mario da Canepina. The interior, a Latin cross with friezes and stucco decoration, is divided into three naves by pillars with pilaster strips in fake marble. The two side naves go round the sacristy, creating an ambulatory, the only one in Rome, recalling the one in Milan cathedral. Its most interesting feature is a fresco in the central vault, the *Fall of the Rebel Angels*, by Giacinto Brandi. The altarpiece, the *Glory of Sts Ambrose and Charles*, was painted by Maratta in 1690. Behind the altar is a reliquary with the heart of St Charles Borromeo. The left transept leads to the sixteenth-century oratory of St Ambrose, built above the church of San Niccolò del Tufo.

SAN LORENZO IN LUCINA ㉑

16/a Via in Lucina
M Spagna
🚌 81, 115, 204, 492, 590, 628

The epithet 'in Lucina' comes from the name of the Roman matron who sheltered Pope St Marcellus (308–309) when he was being persecuted by the Emperor Maxentius. Her house was situated in an area that was important in Imperial Rome, near the temple of Hadrian (Piazza di Pietra), the temple of the Sun (now lost) and the Ara Pacis Augustae, later moved to the Lungotevere. The church was built on the ruins of the house, about the fourth century. Pope St Damasus was elected in it in 366, and it was restored in 685 by Benedict II, in 780 by Adrian I and 1112 by Paschal II, who completely rebuilt it, adding the Romanesque bell-tower whose top three storeys have double mullioned windows. In 1650 Cosimo Fanzago extensively restored the interior. He left almost intact the façade of Paschal II, with the columns of its portico bearing medieval plaques and marble fragments, and its doorway flanked by lions supporting pillars. There is a single nave with side chapels, and in the apse, the marble throne of Paschal II. The coffered ceiling dates from 1857 (Pope Pius IX). On the high altar, which has six Corinthian columns of black marble and a curved tympanum above, is Guido Reni's painting of *Christ on the Cross*. In an urn below the altar is preserved the gridiron on which St Lawrence was martyred. The fourth chapel on the right was designed in the seventeenth century by Gian Lorenzo Bernini, who also made the bust of the doctor Gabriele Fonseca. To the left of the entrance is the baptistery, a jewel of seventeenth-century architecture and decoration, by Sardi.

SANTO SPIRITO IN SASSIA ㉒

12 Via dei Penitenzieri
Ⓜ *Ottaviano - San Pietro*
🚌 *62, 810, 982*

The church of Santo Spirito in Sassia, annexed to the hospital of the same name, stands on the spot where in Carolingian times King Ine of Wessex built the *Schola Saxonum* (Saxon School), a charitable foundation near St Peter's for Saxon pilgrims.

Originally under authority of the church of Santa Maria in Sassia, it was rebuilt in the twelfth century and again in 1475, when it was jointed to the hospital dedicated to the Holy Spirit and built by Sixtus IV to support poor pilgrims in that year's Jubilee.

Devastated in the sack of Rome in 1527, it was rebuilt between 1538 and 1545 by Antonio da Sangallo the younger, under Pope Paul III. The exterior dates from the time of Sixtus V (1585–1590), but the bell-tower from Sixtus IV (1471–1484). It has a single nave, with ten apsidal chapels round the sides, and has pieces of frescoes by various sixteenth- and seventeenth-century painters. The choir, with an organ of 1547, is of high quality. In the adjacent hospital, which retains its early construction, can still be seen the rotating hatch where foundling babies were left.

CHIESA NUOVA ㉓

134 Via del Governo Vecchio
Ⓜ *Spagna*
🚌 *46, 62, 64*

The original building, probably founded by Gregory the Great in the sixth century, stood on a depression in the ground, where bogs and ponds formed. In antiquity it was called Tarentum, and a wide-mouthed cave was believed to be the entrance to hell. In 1575,

honour of his father-in-law Augustus, and dedicated to the dynastic gods of the Julio-Claudian family: Mars, Venus and Julius Caesar. It was rebuilt in its present form in the time of Hadrian.

The Emperor had an inscription in bronze letters placed on the architrave, recording the first builder, Marcus Agrippa. A vestibule with eight granite columns, surmounted by a tympanum originally ornamented with a crowned eagle, leads through a bronze door (the original, but heavily restored), into the circular interior, which gives the Pantheon its popular name, the 'Rotonda'. It is covered by a coffered concrete dome that becomes lighter towards the top,

where pumice was used. With a diameter of 43.30 metres, it is the largest masonry dome ever built. To lighten the weight, the walls are interrupted by blind arches, which can be seen clearly from outside. The interior walls are broken by rectangular and semi-circular niches framed by polychrome marble columns. The upper part of the walls, and the floor, are also in marble, making a powerful visual impact.

Santa Maria sopra Minerva 🟢

35 Via del Beato Angelico
Ⓜ *Barberini*
🚌 *81, 115, 116, 492, 628*

The church of Santa Maria sopra Minerva,

near the Pantheon, dominates the Piazza della Minerva. It was built at the end of the third or the first half of the fourth century, on the ruins of a temple, probably dedicated to Minerva Chalcidica. Its many works of art include the fresco decoration of the Carafa Chapel, in the right-hand part of the transept, with the *Annunciation* and *Assumption* of Filippino Lippi, painted between 1488 and 1493. In the sanctuary we may admire Michelangelo's statue of the *Risen Christ*, of 1519–1520, and in the left-hand part is the slab from the tomb of Fra Angelico, by Isaia da Pisa.

Sant'Ignazio ㉚

8/a Via del Caravita
Ⓜ Barberini
🚌 81, 115, 116, 492, 628

The church, built between 1626 and 1650, dominates the piazza enclosed by the two small palaces designed by Filippo Raguzzini in 1728, forming one of the most characteristic ensembles of eighteenth-century urban planning. It was designed by the Jesuit Father Orazio Grassi, at a time when the Jesuits were at the height of their prestige, because of the recent canonization of Ignatius. The church is a logical complement to the church of Gesù, with parallels to it in the late seventeenth-century façade, by Alessandro Algardi, with its two storeys of Corinthian columns and pilaster strips, and cornices, frontispiece, side volutes, large window and tympanum, all in strong chiaroscuro. There are also similarities in the interior, with its wide nave and apse dominating a Latin-cross plan whose impact is modified by the Baroque decoration and the sumptuousness of the altars in the transept.

The fresco painting of the great vault of the nave, of 1685, is the largest and most accomplished work of Andrea Pozzo. It shows the *Glory of St Ignatius*, entering Paradise where he is welcomed by Christ and the Virgin. A ray of light strikes him, splitting so that it reaches the four corners of the world, and the effect of perspective creates an illusion of open colonnades through which the sky can be seen. Just as spectacular is the impact of the false dome painted by Pozzo on a canvas 17 metres across.

Church of Gesù ㉛

16 Via degli Astalli
Ⓜ Barberini
🚌 81, 116

St Ignatius Loyola was born at the end of fifteenth century and in 1537 founded the Society of Jesus, which Paul III transformed into the Jesuit order. Since their first church (Santa Maria della Strada, behind Palazzo Venezia) was very small, Ignatius wished to build another, to be dedicated to the Holy Name of Jesus. It was to become the prototype for churches between the Counter-Reformation and the Baroque, imitated in Italy and abroad. Work was suspended in 1551 and again in 1554, but, on the death of St Ignatius in 1556, his fellow-Jesuit Francis Borgia handed the project over to Vignola. Work was started in 1568, taking account of St Charles Borromeo's 'Instructions on religious building works'. He believed the artist should serve the priest, and interpret his ideas as dictated by the liturgy and the new demands of worship. When Vignola died, work continued under Giacomo Della Porta, to whom we owe the octagonal drum of dome and the façade, the earliest example of Counter-Reformation architecture. Vignola's interior is stunning for

with splendid frescoes, often conceived as bold compositions that lengthen spaces and create illusionistic settings. In 1679 Baciccia painted a fresco of this kind on the vault, using the technique of overhead perspective that seems to break through the vault. The Chapel of St Ignatius, who is buried beneath the altar in the left transept, is by Andrea Pozzo, built between 1695 and 1699 and richly decorated in marble, bronze and precious stones.

SAN MARCELLO AL CORSO 32

5 Piazza di San Marcello
M *Barberini*
56, 60, 62, 85, 95, 117

Legend has it that Pope St Marcellus (308–309), sentenced by Maxentius to look after the horses at the station of the Imperial mail on the Via Lata (now Via del Corso), was freed by the people and hidden in the nearby house of the matron Lucina, which became a place of pilgrimage. He was arrested again by the Emperor and imprisoned in the same stables, and died in 309. Boniface I was consecrated Pope in the early church in 418. It was restored by Adrian I in the eighth century, and the battered body of Cola di Rienzo was hung up in the apse in 1354. Only the outer walls and the fifteenth-century wooden crucifix from the high altar, now kept in the chapel of the same name, survived the fire of 1519. Money collected to restore the church was used in 1527 to persuade Charles V not to plunder it. It was given its present form in 1592, by Antonio Sangallo the younger, to a design by Jacopo

the grandeur of its conception, and for its bare, unadorned spaciousness. It has a single grand nave with a short transept, flanked by side chapels, focusing all attention on the high altar, visible from all parts of the church. It combined simplicity with the need for a more active deepening of faith through ritual and preaching. Nevertheless, with Vignola's death the relationship between the body of the church and the façade changed. The Baroque decoration added later transformed the initial concept, replacing bare plaster

Sansovino that removed the side naves and transept. The concave façade of 1682 is by Carlo Fontana; the doorway is flanked by three columns on each side, supporting a curvilinear tympanum. The upper level is tied to the lower by two palm leaves. The curve of this façade increases the visual impact of its architectural elements, in harmony with the sculpture of Antonio Raggi, from 1686. The interior has a single nave, with five chapels on each side, and frescoes by G. B. Ricci of Novara. Under the altar is a third-century marble memorial stone, decorated on the front with twelfth-century *opus sectile* mosaic and used to contain martyrs' relics.

SANTI APOSTOLI ㉝

Piazza Santi Apostoli
M *Barberini*
56, 60, 62, 85, 95, 117

Although an early building is believed to date back to Pope Julius I (337–352), the church was founded by Pelagius I (556–561) after the Goths were driven out, and John III (561– 574) completed it and dedicated it to the Apostles James and Philip. The ancient church contained an image of the Saviour painted by Melozzo da Forlì, which Clement XI had transferred to the Quirinal Palace. In the sanctuary was a tabernacle of the Eucharist, and on the high altar, the *tegurium*, a canopy supported on four porphyry columns. It was restored by Stephen V (885–891), but Pope Martin V (Colonna) was responsible for reconstructing it in 1417, after it had fallen into ruin and been abandoned following an earthquake in 1348. The whole of the surrounding area

belonged to the Colonna family, including the palace, in which the Pope stayed for a time while the Lateran Palace was being repaired. It had been built to mark the restoration of the church, considered almost a family chapel. At the end of the 1400s, the architect Baccio Pontelli, in the service of Pope Sixtus IV, transformed the façade, creating the loggia with nine arches on two levels, of which the upper was later walled up by Carlo Rainaldi in the second half of the seventeenth century. He conceived the Baroque windows and the balustrade with statues of Christ and the twelve Apostles. It was restored again by Carlo and Francesco Fontana under Clement XI (1700– 1721), and in 1827 Valadier designed its present plain, very tall neo-classical façade with its huge central window and tympanum. From the sixteenth century the name of the basilica was extended to include all the Apostles.

Under the portico there is one of the most beautiful Imperial Roman eagles, from the first century A.D., a rather fine lion supporting a pillar, signed by Vassalletto, from the thirteenth century, and early Christian fragments and tombstones.

The interior is divided into three naves by large pillars with matching Corinthian pilaster strips; it has three domed chapels on each side, and is full of works of art. On the vault of the central nave is a fresco by Baciccia, showing the *Triumph of the Order of St Francis*, of 1707, and above the sanctuary, one by G. Odazzi, of the *Expulsion of the Rebel Angels*, of 1709. On the far wall is a canvas by D. Muratori, depicting the *Martyrdom of Sts Philip and James*. The Chapel of the Crucifixion, to the right of the apse, is divided into three small naves by eight spiral columns from the original church. Two sixteenth-century cloisters complete the church complex. To the left of the basilica stands the fifteenth-century Santi Apostoli Palace, belonging to the Holy See, with corner towers and marble windows, possibly built by Giuliano da Sangallo in 1478 for the future Pope Julius II.

SANTA MARIA DI LORETO

26 Piazza di Santa Maria di Loreto

M *Colosseo*

🚌 *56, 60, 62, 64, 85, 87*

The church was started by Antonio da Sangallo the younger in 1507 and finished by Jacopo del Duca, following the demolition of another church given to the bakers' guild by Pope Alexander VI. Its fifteenth-century altarpiece by Antoniazzo Romano, depicting the *Madonna with St Sebastian and St Roch*, came from that church, and now stands on Onorio Longhi's altar.

The exterior is a cube, and its dome is topped by an unusual lantern, the 'crickets' cage'. The interior is octagonal, with chapels in the niches on the oblique sides, and a deep sanctuary.

SANTISSIMO NOME DI MARIA

89 Foro Traiano

M *Colosseo*

🚌 *56, 60, 62, 64, 85, 87*

On the site of a little fifteenth-century church belonging to the Company of St Bernard was built an even smaller one, in 1683. The present church, on a symmetrical plan, was built next to it in 1736. It has a square foundation with rounded corners, a high drum and a dome in eight sections. In the elliptical interior are seven small chapels, decorated in polychrome marble, and an image of the Virgin, once housed in the oratory of San Lorenzo in Laterano and taken in solemn procession from the now destroyed church of San Bernardo to its present place.

San Marco ㊱

48 Piazza San Marco
Ⓜ Colosseo
🚌 44, 81, 95, 160, 628, 715

This is one of Rome's oldest churches, probably founded by Pope Marcus in 336, on the spot where St Mark is said to have lived while he was in Rome. It was on the basilical plan, with an orientation similar to today's. In the fifth century it was destroyed and rebuilt, facing in the opposite direction. In the sixth and seventh centuries it was repeatedly sacked by Goths, Lombards and Byzantines. It was rebuilt by Adrian I (772–795), with its present orientation, but immediately flooded when the Tiber broke its banks

in 791. Gregory IV (827–844) restored it, adding the mosaics in the apse, and in 1100 it acquired its bell-tower and a now lost canopy.

Cardinal Pietro Barbo, who became Pope Paul II (1464–1471), transformed it, turning it into the church of the Venetians in Rome and the most interesting building from the beginning of the Roman Renaissance. The façade is by Leon Battista Alberti, who was at that time in the service of the papal court. It has a portico of three arches, marked by vigorous piers with half-columns

back to back. The very elegant Loggia of Benedictions above it, with broader arches and slender pilaster strips, was completed by Giuliano da Maiano in 1471. Paul II then had his residence built next to the church. It was called Palazzo Venezia because it was the residence of the Venetian ambassadors. Under the portico in front of the church are the Renaissance door of Isaia da Pisa, remains of the ancient canopy and a curious inscription on a medieval well-head, cursing anyone who sold the water drawn from it. The fifteenth-century interior has three naves, and a wooden ceiling from the second half of the century, possibly the oldest in Rome, with that of Santa Maria Maggiore. The ninth-century mosaic in the apse shows Christ blessing, five saints and the donor, Pope Gregory V. Under the mullioned windows of Paul II, in the central nave, are eighteenth-century frescoes and the funerary monument of the child Leonardo Pesaro, by Antonio Canova (1796). On the altar of Pietro da Cortona's Chapel of the

Sacrament is the portrait of Pope St Marcus by Melozzo da Forlì. His portrait of St Mark the Evangelist is in the sacristy, where there are also traces of a fresco of the school of Cavallini.

ORATORY OF THE SANTISSIMO SACRAMENTO

11 Piazza Poli
M *Barberini*
🚍 *56, 58, 60, 62, 81, 85*

Built by order of the brotherhood of the same name during the papacy of Gregory XIII (1572–1585), it was completed in 1681 with the addition of the façade, by Carlo Rainaldi. Under Benedict XIII (1724–1730) it was completely reconstructed by Gregorini, with its present interior decoration. The outside of the doorway has two pairs of half-columns supporting a broken curvilinear pediment, surmounted by statues representing *Faith* and *Hope*. The interior, which is elliptical, with a dome, has on its walls pairs of fluted pilaster strips under a large projecting cornice. The eighteenth-century *Holy Family* on the altar is by Trevisani.

SANTA MARIA IMMACOLATA A VIA VENETO 🔢

27 Via Veneto
M *Barberini*
🚍 *95, 116, 204*

The church, known also as Santa Maria della Concezione and Chiesa dei Cappuccini, has a single nave with ten side-chapels. It was built to a design by Antonio Casoni from 1626 to 1631, but the façade and the steps in front were altered in the twentieth century. The first chapel on the right contains two paintings, Guido Reni's *Archangel Michael* (1630) (see illustration) and *Christ Mocked*, by Gherardo

Delle Notti. Also worth noting are *St Francis with the Stigmata*, by Domenichino and the tomb (1646) of Cardinal Antonio Barberini, who funded the church, with its famous inscription 'Here lie dust and ashes, nothing else'. In the convent are Caravaggio's *St Francis* (1603) and the *Nazarene*, by Jacopo Palma the younger. The adjacent cemetery of the Capuchins has five chapels made up of the bones and skulls of 4,000 friars who died between 1528 and 1870.

SANT'ANDREA AL QUIRINALE ❸⓿

29 Via del Quirinale
Ⓜ Barberini
▥ 71, 115, 117

In 1658, Cardinal
Pamphilj, nephew of
Pope Innocent X, paid for
a church to be built for
the adjoining Jesuit
convent. Bernini was put
in charge, and work was
completed thirteen years
later. The façade consists
of a single storey, with a
semicircular vestibule
supported on two
columns and flanked by
two tall pilaster strips
which support the
tympanum. The interior is
elliptical in shape,
decorated with gilded
stucco and marble. Four
chapels and four deep
niches open off the
central area; they contain
seventeenth- and
eighteenth-century
paintings. The dome is
coffered and gilded, and
decorated with friezes and
stucco. Under the altar is
a bronze and lapis lazuli
urn, containing the saint's
body.

SAN CARLO ALLE QUATTRO FONTANE ❹⓿

23 Via del Quirinale
Ⓜ Barberini
▥ 60, 61, 62, 175, 492

This church stands at
the junction of the
Strada Felice, opened
by Pope Sixtus V in
1586, and the Strada
Pia, constructed on the
orders of Pope Pius IV
in 1565. In 1634
Borromini was
commissioned to build
a monastery and
church for the
Spanish Discalced
Trinitarians. He
first built the
cloisters, then the
church, dedicated
to the Holy Trinity
and St Charles
Borromeo, and
now better known
as San Carlino alle
Quattro Fontane.
In 1664 work
began on the
celebrated façade,
finished after
Borromini's death
in 1667 by his
nephew Bernardo.

The great architect has
brilliantly solved the
problems of having to
work on a restricted site
and place his building
at the junction of two
streets. The façade is
closely integrated with
the convent, which
continues beyond the
corner, giving an
unusual diagonal view
of the church which
includes the façade, the
convent and the
fountain on the corner,
with its pointed
campanile. The façade
is on two superimposed
levels, curved in the
shape of a double S,
convex in the centre
and concave on the two
wings. Above the
doorway is a niche,

crowned by a tympanum formed of the outspread wings of two angels. On the upper part is a rich, curving pavilion on a small balcony flanked by four columns aligned with those below, terminating in a tilted oval lucarne supported by two flying angels. The lantern of the elliptical dome is made up of four concave niches separated by small columns. The interior, on an elliptical plan, with its major axis lengthways, also creates a sense of contraction, as against expansion. The single order of columns deliberately creates a sense of disproportion in a space whose surfaces are forced to curve. The dome, squeezed and distorted by the tangential curves of the arches, is decorated with octagonal, hexagonal and cruciform coffers. A chapel in the crypt was set aside for Borromini, who committed suicide in 1667, but it remains empty.

SANTA MARIA DELLA VITTORIA ④

17 Via XX Settembre
M *Barberini*
🚌 *60, 61, 62, 175, 492*

The first claim to fame of this church is Gian Lorenzo Bernini's masterpiece, the *Ecstasy of St Teresa*, completed in 1646 and placed in the Cornaro Chapel. In an almost theatrical setting, the donor, Cardinal Francesco Cornaro, and his family witness the saint's ecstasy, as she lies on a cloud, her mouth and eyes half closed. In front of her, an angel holding a dart is about to pierce her heart, after a passage in the *Life* of St Teresa. This altarpiece demonstrates Bernini's innovation in handling his subject: the viewer is an involuntary witness of the extraordinary event.

Scenes from the life of the saint of Avila are depicted on the vault in gilded stucco relief. The victory to which the name of the church refers is that won in 1620 by Ferdinand II Habsburg, thanks to a miraculous image of Mary found in Bohemia. The church was therefore built in the first half of the seventeenth century; it was designed by Carlo Maderno. The interior shows its Baroque style, with its rich marble and the ornamentation of its single nave and six side chapels. In one of them can be seen the last canvases painted in Rome by Domenichino, *The Ecstasy of St Francis* and *St Francis Receiving the Stigmata*, dated 1630. In the third chapel on the left is Guercino's *Holy Trinity*, painted about 1642.

Santa Maria degli Angeli 42

9 Via Cernale
M *Repubblica*
▥ *60, 61, 62, 175, 492*

Giuliano da Sangallo and Baldasarre Peruzzi had had the idea of transforming the Baths of Diocletian but it was not until 1561, under Pius IV, that the rooms of the baths were consecrated to the angels and the Christian martyrs who, legend tells, were employed in building the Roman complex. Michelangelo was commissioned to carry out the project, and produced a building that was almost a Greek cross. Further alterations in the eighteenth century were completed by Luigi Vanvitelli for the Holy Year of 1750, giving the basilica its present form. The sixteenth-century façade was demolished in the twentieth century, in order to expose the Roman walls. In the vestibule, converted from the old *calidarium* or hot room, are the funerary monuments of the painters Carlo Maratta and Salvator Rosa, and of Cardinal Francesco Alciati, by Giovanni Battista Della Porta. The transverse nave is formed from the old *tepidarium*, or cool room, covered by three groin-vaults resting on huge monolithic granite columns. In the sanctuary is Domenichino's *Martyrdom of St Sebastian* (1629) and Giovanni Francesco Romanelli's *Presentation of Mary in the Temple* (1640).

Santa Prassede 43

9/a Via di Santa Prassede
M *Cavour*
▥ *4, 9, 16, 75, 204, 590, 714*

This was an old *titulus* or parish church, going back at least to the fifth century and dedicated to the figure of Praxedes, who according to tradition was the sister of Pudentiana and daughter of the senator Pudens, who is said to have entertained St Paul.

Very little remains today of the early Christian church, which was completely rebuilt by Pope Paschal I (817–824), who transferred to it from the catacombs the remains of about two thousand martyrs.

Further changes and additions were made in the sixteenth century, and the sanctuary area and the crypt were rebuilt in the eighteenth. The magnificent ninth-century mosaic in the apse shows, below the monogram of Paschal I, the Saviour with Sts Peter and Paul, Pudentiana and Praxedes, St Zeno, and the Pope as donor. Below, the Mystical Lamb on the mountain of Paradise is flanked by twelve sheep, symbolizing the Apostles, who are leaving Jerusalem and Bethlehem. The triumphal arch and the arch of the apse are decorated with other mosaics of the same period. The right-hand nave leads to the cruciform Chapel of St Zeno, covered in mosaics and a gem of Byzantine art in Rome.

It was dedicated by Paschal I to his mother, Theodora, who is buried here. In a small side room is the pillar of the scourging, brought from Jerusalem in 1223, and considered a relic of Christ's Passion.

San Pietro in Vincoli 🀤

4/a Piazza San Pietro in Vincoli
M *Cavour*
🚌 *4, 9, 16, 75, 204, 590, 714*

The basilica, also known as the Eudoxiana, stands on the ruins of an Imperial villa, on which Eudoxia, wife of the Emperor Valentinian III,

had a basilica built in the fifth century as a place to keep the chains in which St Peter was held captive in Jerusalem. Legend has it that they were miraculously welded with those used to imprison the saint in the Mamertine prison in Rome, which are now preserved under the nineteenth-century high altar. The church was consecrated by Pope Sixtus III (432–440), restored by Adrian I (772–795) and strengthened in the eleventh century, after the Norman invasion. Between 1471 and 1503, the future Pope Julius II, Cardinal Giuliano della Rovere, had the side naves and transept covered by a groin-vault, and the portico entirely rebuilt. It was raised in the seventeenth century, hiding the old façade, and is now spoiled by

the modern Via Cavour. The interior has three naves, with a seventeenth-century fresco by Parodi on the ceiling of the central one. Other features include a seventh-century Byzantine mosaic, depicting St Sebastian, a *Deposition of Christ* by Pomarancio, in the first altar in the left-hand nave, and paintings by Guercino and Domenichino in the right-hand nave. The most famous work of art is Michelangelo's *Moses*, part of the proposed memorial of Julius II, a grandiose work intended for St Peter's in the Vatican.

This statue is extraordinarily powerful, exuding superhuman energy and strength of character, in keeping with the sculptor's vehement and passionate nature.

SANTI QUATTRO CORONATI 🐵

20 Via dei Santi Quattro
M *Colosseo*
🚌 *85, 117, 850*

The church was founded by Pope Melchiades (311–314) to honour the Four Crowned Martyrs, Severus, Severianus, Carpophorus and Victorinus, who refused to worship an idol of the god Aesculapius. It is also dedicated to the five Pannonian stone-cutters who declined a request to carve the idol. Pope Leo IV (625–638) brought their relics to the church. Honorius I (625–638) restored it, but it was destroyed in the sack of Rome by the Normans in 1084 and restored again by Pope Paschal II (1099–1118), who created three naves from the single central one. The left-hand nave was then demolished to make way for the cloisters, and the right-hand one turned

into a refectory. In 1521 the church, administered by the Benedictines since the twelfth century, passed into the hands of the Camaldolese and in 1560 to the Augustinians, who are still responsible for it. The complex resembles a kind of 'fortified convent', a defensive bastion for St John Lateran. In fact, it stands on the edge of the route of the papal procession from the Lateran to the Vatican. The apse closes off the three naves, since it is part of the old church; it has a fresco by Giovanni da San Giovanni.

The skull of St Sebastian is preserved in the left-hand altar. A door in the left-hand nave leads to the Romanesque cloisters. In the Chapel of St Sylvester are frescoes of 1246, depicting scenes from the life of the saint and the *Legend of Constantine*, and in the portico between the two courtyards there is one of the *Last Judgement*.

SANCTUARY OF THE MADONNA DEL DIVINO AMORE 🐵

Via Ardeatina Km. 12
🚌 *218 from San Giovanni in Laterano, 702 from P.le Ostiense*

'Rome's new Marian Sanctuary, alongside its oldest, Santa Maria Maggiore' is how John Paul II described this shrine. Since 1740, the year when the first miracle occurred, pilgrims have been coming here to renew their faith, calling on the intercession of the Virgin Mary. To ward off the city's destruction during World War II, Romans made a votive offering at the shrine. It has been included in the official itinerary for pilgrims in Holy Year, and is a place where they obtain indulgences.

APIDES VIVI (1 Peter 2:5)

Living stones

Spiritual Message

One of the reasons for a pilgrimage is to discover the face of God as witnessed within the churches, and how these remind us of how God, through Jesus Christ, unfolds the history of salvation offered to all. Going on a visit to these churches means to pause a little and gain sustenance for the journey. The churches within the city are living signs of communities who have experienced God in their lives, and remind us that a world without God is a world without meaning. These are places where the Word of God is proclaimed, heard and celebrated in the Sacraments.

When a sacrament is celebrated in the Church, a meeting takes place between the person, Christ and the Holy Spirit. Life takes on a different meaning. Thus, when the pilgrim sets on his or her journey to meet God, there is an awareness that the whole Church is on pilgrimage towards the heavenly Jerusalem. While it is true that we are all pilgrims towards that future city, it is also our duty, as 'living stones for a spiritual house' (1 Peter 2:5), to be committed to a society which is more just and human. That is why during this journey we need to learn to be part of the Church marked with joy and hope. Whoever enters a church or a sanctuary knows that God does not remain there simply to watch our lot, but he is actively present in it. The churches represent this presence of God in history. Visiting these churches, the pilgrim lets his or her heart be open to the marvels of the grace of the Holy Spirit, and through the Word and the Sacraments gets closer to the sense of God and the habit of prayer. And when it happens that people forget to speak of God, let these 'stones which have pleased your servants' (Psalm 102:15) continue to speak of him.

VIII

CHURCHES
OF THE WORLD'S
CATHOLICS

ATIONES EX LONGINQUO
AD TE VENIENT (Tobit 13:13)

*Many nations will come
to you from far away*

Spiritual Introduction

*The Church of Rome, centre of communion around the
successor of Peter, recalls the original unity of the Church.
'Full of light, she radiates her rays on the whole world, but
there is only one light that shines everywhere without dividing
its unity. In fact, the Church spreads her branches widely over
all the earth. Her smoothly running waters pour out in all
latitudes. But there is only one trunk, only one spring, only
one fecund Mother from whose womb we came forth. We
were nourished by her milk. We were given life by her soul.'
(St Cyprian, De Ecclesiae Unitate, 5, 6). If 'the Church of
Christ is united by a bond of charity' (Peter Damian, Liber qui
appellatur 'Dominus Vobiscum', 5, 6), 'the Church of Rome
presides over the union of charity' of all Churches (St Ignatius
of Antioch, To the Romans). The primacy deriving from Peter
and Paul makes her the cradle of the apostolic tradition. She
is 'the greatest and most ancient Church, known to all,
founded and established in Rome by the two glorious Apostles
Peter and Paul... With this Church, by virtue of her most
excellent origin, every Church, i.e., the faithful coming from
everywhere, must come in agreement. In fact, the tradition
that comes from the Apostles is conserved in her for all men
and women' (Irenaeus, Adversus haereses, 3, 3, 2). 'But the
Church, that is spread among all peoples, speaks in everyone's*

200

*The Church Gathered from Israel and
the Church Gathered from the Gentiles*, Santa Sabina, Rome

tongue' (St Augustine, Commentary on John, *32, 7). The
unity of the Catholic, i.e. universal, Church, is enriched, not
divided, by the different talents and insights of the individual
Churches. The national churches in Rome represent the local
Churches purely by their presence, as a sign of communion
with the See of Peter. If 'the holy Church is the Body of Christ,
thus only one Spirit vivifies her, unites her in only one faith
and sanctifies her, (if) the members of this body are the
individual faithful, and all form only one body, thanks to the
one Spirit and the one faith that bind them together' (Hugh of
St Victor,* De Sacramentis Christianae Fidei, *II, 2), then the
Spirit that keeps the bond of faith among all the faithful and
all the Churches, blossoms in the national churches. A sign of
Catholic unity – unity in diversity – they are also a prayer to
the Holy Spirit for unity: of the Catholic Church, of all
Christians, of all people. By simply being in Rome, the various
faithful of different nationalities, who have come from far
away (Tobit 13:11) are a mute and eloquent ecumenical
prayer, a peaceful coexistence of different cultures
acknowledging in Peter the unity of the faith.*

Churches of the World's Catholics

The map shows the location of the various national Catholic churches in Rome described in detail on pages 204–210.

Historical Notes

SANT'ANTONIO ABATE ALL'ESQUILINO (RUSSIA)

BYZANTINE-RUSSIAN RITE

2 Via Carlo Alberto
Ⓜ Vittorio Emanuele
🚌 4, 70, 71

In 1259, Cardinal Pietro Capocci decided to build a hospital near the early Christian church of St Andrew *Cata Barbara* (or *in Piscinula*), built in the fifth century on the site of the fourth-century pagan residence of Julius Bassus. The hospital was named after the church, and in 1289, the name was added of St John of Jerusalem of the Antonines. The fine Romanesque doorway by the Vassalletto family, facing Via Carlo Alberto, is a remnant of the medieval building. In 1308, the Antonines founded a new church, dedicated to St Antony Abbot, which underwent many alterations over the centuries. Inside, the frescoes by Pomarancio and the chapel of St Antony are interesting. By the end of the sixteenth century, the buildings had been surrounded by a wall, and the old St Antony's church had fallen into ruin. The church acquired its present appearance in the early 1700s. On 17 January, the feast day of St Antony, considered the patron saint of animals, horses and carts would be solemnly blessed outside it. In 1928, the Holy See acquired the whole site, to build four pontifical institutes, and the church was included in one of them, the Pontifical Russian Institute. In 1932 it was handed over to Russian Catholics of the Byzantine-Slavonic rite and the interior was slightly altered to create an iconostasis and adapt it to the Byzantine liturgy.

SANTO STEFANO ROTONDO AL CELIO (HUNGARY) ❷

Via di Santo Stefano Rotondo
(See p. 175)

SANTI SERGIO E BACCO OR MADONNA DEL PASCOLO (UKRAINE)

BYZANTINE-UKRAINIAN RITE ❸

3 Piazza Madonna dei Monti
Ⓜ Cavour
🚌 115

The Ukrainian church is in the heart of the Monti quarter. It is recorded as early as the ninth century and owes its present form to its reconstruction by the eighteenth-century architect Francesco Ferrari. The façade dates from 1896.

SANTA MARIA IN COSMEDIN

BYZANTINE-GREEK-MELCHITE RITE ❹

18 Piazza Bocca della Verità
(See p. 174)

Sant'Antonio Abate all'Esquilino

San Stanislao alle Botteghe Oscure (Poland) ❺

15 Via delle Botteghe Oscure
🚌 44, 46, 170, 186

The first church on this site, dedicated to the Saviour *Pensilis de Surraca,* is mentioned in a document in 1174.
In 1582, Gregory XIII granted it to the Polish Cardinal Stanislaus Hosius, who rebuilt it and dedicated it to St Stanislas, Bishop of Krakow, martyred in 1079 and Poland's patron saint. The Polish church, with its attached hospice, was completely rebuilt in 1753.

San Giuliano dei Fiamminghi (Belgium) ❻

40 Via del Sudario
🚌 8, 44, 64, 70, 115

Tradition has it that this little church was founded when Flanders converted to the faith, in the papacy of Gregory II (715–753).
It is known for its fine Baroque façade, with, above the door, a statue of St Julian the Hospitaller, a saint of unknown nationality adopted by the Belgians as their patron and believed to come from Ath, in Hainaut.

Santa Brigida a Campo de' Fiori

Santa Brigida a Campo de' Fiori (Sweden) ❼

96 Piazza Farnese
🚌 62, 64, 116

The oldest church goes back to the time of Boniface IX (1389–1404). It was left abandoned until Pope Paul III (1534–1549) granted it to the Bishop of Uppsala, Olaus Magnus. With its hospice, it was later entrusted to the Convertite sisters. It was comprehensively restored in the eighteenth century.

Nostra Signora di Guadalupe e San Filippo martire in Via Aurelia (Mexico) ❽

675 Via Aurelia
🚌 246

This parish church was built in 1960 and is in the care of the Missionaries of the Sacred Heart of Jesus (Legionaries of Christ).

Santa Sofia (Ukraine)
Byzantine-Ukrainian rite ❾

478 Via Boccea
🚌 904, 905, 906

When Cardinal Josyf Slipyj, Metropolitan of the Ukrainian Catholic Church, returned from his twenty-year exile in Siberia, he had this church built in 1967–1968. It is called the *Sober,* meaning Mother Church or meeting place for special festivals, of Holy Wisdom, and is the spiritual and religious centre for all Ukrainians. On 28 September 1976, Pope Paul VI brought the relics of Pope St Clement (88–97) to the church. It has a wonderful iconostasis, painted by Juvenalij Josyf Mokryckyj.

SANTO STEFANO DEGLI ABISSINI

(ETHIOPIA) COPTIC RITE

Vatican City

🚌 904, 905, 906

The church was built by Pope Leo III (795–816), who named it St Stephen's the Greater. In 1479 it was assigned by Sixtus IV to the Coptic monks. Under Clement XI (1700–1721) it was quite radically altered. It has a notable doorway, with the Lamb and the cross, from the twelfth century.

SANTI MICHELE E MAGNO (NETHERLANDS) ⓫

Borgo Santo Spirito

Ⓜ Ottaviano, San Pietro
🚌 62, 810, 982

This church, known as the 'Church of the Friesians', was, in the Middle Ages, part of the 'School of the Friesians', where pilgrims coming to Rome from Holland gathered. The present church dates from 1141 and was restored in 1756. From the 15th century it belonged to the Fabric of St. Peter's and was entrusted to the Archconfraternity of the Most Holy Sacrament. Since 1989 the Dutch community has used the church on Sundays.

SAN GIOSAFAT AL GIANICOLO (UKRAINE) ⓬

4 Passeggiata del Gianicolo
🚌 870

This is the church attached to the Pontifical Ukrainian College of St Josaphat, founded in 1897.

SANTA MARIA IN MONSERRATO DEGLI SPAGNOLI (SPAIN) ⓭

151 Via Giulia
🚌 116

Built in 1518, to designs by Antonio da Sangallo the younger, with a façade of pilaster strips by Francesco da Volterra, it stands on the site of a complex belonging to the Catalans. Alexander VI, the Borgia Pope (1492–1503), established a Spanish national fraternity in the church, under the protection of

Santa Maria in Monserrato degli Spagnoli

the Virgin of Montserrat. The church contains the tombs of the Borgia Popes Callixtus III (1455–1458) and Alexander VI, which were removed from St Peter's when the new basilica was built. A room next to the church contains a portrait of Cardinal Pedro Montoya, one of the earliest works of Gian Lorenzo Bernini.

SAN TOMMASO IN PARIONE (ETHIOPIA) COPTIC RITE ⓮

33 Via del Parione
🚌 46, 62, 64, 70, 81, 87, 115, 492, 628

The church was consecrated by Pope Innocent II in 1139, and rebuilt in 1582 to a design by Francesco da Volterra.

SANTA MARIA DELL'ANIMA (GERMANY) ⓯

20 Via della Pace
🚌 46, 62, 64, 70, 81, 87, 115, 492, 628

The church stands on the site of the chapel of the hospice for pilgrims from Germany and the Low Countries, and was rebuilt in the early 1500s. Its fine façade is attributed to Giuliano da Sangallo. The three doors, and the *Madonna and Two Souls*, which gives the church its name, have recently been attributed to Sansovino. It was completely restored in 1843. It contains many works of art from different periods, by Italian, Flemish and German artists. Of special interest is *The Holy Family and Saints*, by Giulio Romano (1522), in the sanctuary.

Santa Maria in Campo Marzio

SAN LUIGI DEI FRANCESI (FRANCE) ⑯

5 Piazza San Luigi dei Francesi
(See p. 186)

SANT'ANTONIO IN CAMPO MARZIO (PORTUGAL) ⑰

2 Via dei Portoghesi
🚌 46

The earliest church, going back to 1440, was built by Cardinal Martin de Chavez in a predominantly Portuguese neighbourhood. It was rebuilt in 1630, with an ornate Baroque façade by Martino Longhi. The colourful interior is by Carlo Rainaldi and Cristoforo Schor. The monument of Alexander de Souza, by Antonio Canova, and the paintings by Nicolas Lorrain and Antoniazzo Romano are of interest.

SAN SALVATORE ALLE COPPELLE (ROMANIA) BYZANTINE-ROMANIAN RITE ⑱

72/b Piazza delle Coppelle
🚌 116

A stone inside the church, mentioning Celestine III (1190–1198), who was responsible for the bell-tower, suggests that it dates from before 1195. It was rebuilt in 1700.

SANTA MARIA DELLA CONCEZIONE IN CAMPO MARZIO (SYRIA) SYRIAN-ANTIOCHENE RITE ⑲

45 Piazza Campo Marzio
🚌 81, 115, 116, 117, 492, 628

Pious legend would have us believe that the nuns of the convent of St Anastasia in Constantinople fled to Rome in 750 to escape persecution by the iconoclasts under the Emperors Leo III and Constantine V, bringing with them the body of St Gregory Nazianzene. In Rome, Pope Zacharias is supposed to have had a convent built for them in the Campus Martius, where they built two churches, one dedicated to Mary, the other to St Gregory Nazianzene. The church of Santa Maria della Concezione was first enlarged by Giacomo della Porta in 1564, and again, in its entirety, by Giovanni Antonio De Rossi, in 1685. Inside, it is a Greek cross, with a dome. Over the high altar is a painting dating from the twelfth or thirteenth century, showing the Virgin as Advocate.

San Girolamo dei Croati (Croatia) 20

132 Via Tomacelli
M *Spagna*
🚌 *81, 115, 628, 926*

When the Turks invaded Illyria, many people fled and found refuge in Rome, possibly in the area where the church of San Girolamo was later built. In 1453, Pope Nicholas V granted them land to build a hospice. The church was rebuilt under Sixtus V by Martino Longhi the elder.

San Atanasio a Via del Babuino (Greece)
Byzantine-Greek rite 21

149 Via del Babuino
🚌 *117*

The church was built by Giacomo della Porta in the papacy of Gregory XIII (1572–1585), when the Greek College was founded. It has a brick façade with two bell-towers. The high altar, in accordance with the Greek rite, is cut off by the wooden iconostasis by Andrea Busiri Vici (1876), which replaces an earlier one. In the apse is a *Crucifixion* by the Cavalier d'Arpino.

San Silvestro in Capite (England) 22

Piazza San Silvestro
🚌 *52, 53, 58, 58, 71, 85, 160, 850*

Paul I (757–767) built a monastery, dedicated to Popes St Sylvester and St Stephen, on the site of the pagan temple of the Sun. The two saints were buried in the adjoining oratory. The complex was called *inter duos hortos* (between two gardens), and also *in capite*, because relics of the head of John the Baptist were kept there. The church was rebuilt in 1198, when the fine bell-tower was added. It acquired its present form between the end of the sixteenth and the beginning of the eighteenth century, from artists such as Francesco da Volterra, Carlo Maderno, Carlo Rainaldi, Mattia and Domenico De Rossi. Its notable works of art include a painting by Orazio Gentileschi and frescoes in the dome by Pomarancio and his co-workers.

Sant'Isidoro a Capo le Case (Ireland) 23

41 Via degli Artisti
M *Barberini*
🚌 *52, 53, 56, 58, 58, 95*

The church and its adjoining college were founded by Ottaviano Vestri di Barbiano, after a papal Bull of Urban VIII in 1525, and entrusted to Irish Reformed Observant

San Silvestro in Capite

Sant'Isidoro

Franciscans. The 1704 portico and façade are by Bizzacheri. It contains paintings by Maratta and some architectural features and sculpture attributed to Bernini. Next to the church is the fine *aula maxima* or main hall of Luke Wadding's college, with important fresco cycles by Fra Emanuele da Como. This was the scene of the famous disputes of the 'Scotist' followers of the philosopher-theologian Duns Scotus (c. 1266–1308).

San Giovanni Marone (Lebanon)
Syrian-Maronite rite

6 Via Aurora
🚌 95, 116

The church, built in 1924, is attached to the Maronite College.

San Nicola da Tolentino agli Orti Sallustiani
(Armenia) Armenian rite ㉕

17 Salita di San Nicola da Tolentino
Ⓜ *Barberini*

Built in 1599, at the wish of Prince Camillo Pamphilj, it was rebuilt in 1614 by the architect Giovanni Maria Baratta. Its Baroque façade, with steps in front, is notable. It adjoins the Pontifical Armenian College.

Santa Susanna alle Terme di Diocleziano
(United States) ㉖

14 Via XX Settembre
🚌 16, 37, 60, 61, 62, 136, 137

The church has gone through numerous phases of development, from ancient times to the seventeenth century. One tradition is that it was where St Susanna was martyred, and the *titulus* of Pope Caius (283–296), brother of Gabinus, her father. Pope Leo III (795–816) had the oldest phase (possibly a large fourth-century church with an apse and internal galleries) decorated with mosaics. It was rebuilt under Sixtus IV, and then by Cardinal Rusticucci between 1593 and 1603, when it was completed by Carlo Maderno.

San Patrizio a Villa Ludovisi (Ireland) ㉗

31 Via Boncompagni
Ⓜ *Barberini*
🚌 52, 53, 56, 58, ~~58~~, 95

Built in the early 1900s in the Nordic Neo-romantic style, to a design by Aristide

Santa Susanna alle Terme di Diocleziano

Leonori. It contains frescoes from the old church of Santa Maria in Posterula, demolished when San Patrizio was built.

NOSTRA SIGNORA DEL SANTISSIMO SACRAMENTO E SANTI MARTIRI CANADESI
(CANADA) Ⓘ

Via Giovanni Battista de Rossi
Ⓜ Policlinico
🚌 9, 490, 495

In 1948 the Generalate of the Blessed Sacrament Fathers acquired a piece of land on which to build a centre, and a parish church was added later. Because Canada had helped to pay for it to be built, it was dedicated to the Martyrs of Canada (1630–1680).

The unusually daring architecture is the work of Bruno Apollonj Ghetti (1955) and the internal furnishings and decoration are by contemporary artists.

SANTA MARIA ADDOLORATA A PIAZZA BUENOS AIRES (ARGENTINA) Ⓙ

81 Viale Regina Margherita
🚌 19, 30

Monsignor José Leon Gallardo laid the first stone of the church of Santa Maria Addolorata on 9 July 1910, the centenary of Argentina's independence. Benedict XV made it the Argentine national church in 1915, and it is administered by the Argentine Bishops' Conference.

Italian regional churches

ABRUZZI
Santa Maria Maddalena in Campo Marzio
56 Piazza della Maddalena

BERGAMO
Santi Bartolomeo ed Alessandro a Piazza Colonna
70 Via di Pietra

BOLOGNA
Santi Giovanni Evangelista e Petronio dei Bolognesi
61 Via del Mascherone

CALABRIA
San Francesco di Paola ai Monti
10 Piazza San Francesco di Paola

CAMERINO
Santi Fabiano e Venanzio
92 Via Terni

FLORENCE
San Giovanni Battista de' Fiorentini
2 Via Acciaioli

GENOA
San Giovanni Battista dei Genovesi
12 Via Anicia

LOMBARDY
Santi Ambrogio e Carlo al Corso
240 Via del Corso

LUCCA
Santa Croce e San Bonaventura alla Pilotta
3 Via dei Lucchesi

MARCHE
See Piceno

NAPLES
Santo Spirito dei Napoletani
34 Via Giulia

NICE
See Piedmont

NORCIA
Santi Benedetto e Scolastica
1 Vicolo Sinibaldi

PICENO AND MARCHE
San Salvatore in Lauro
15 Piazza San Salvatore in Lauro

PIEDMONT
Santissimo Sudario all'Argentina
47 Via del Sudario

APULIA
San Nicola in Carcere
46 Via del Teatro Marcello

SIENA
Santa Caterina da Siena a Via Giulia
111 Via Monserrato

SICILY
Santa Maria Odigitria al Tritone
12 Via Anicia

VENICE
San Marco Evangelista al Campidoglio
48 Piazza San Marco

N OMNI CONVERSATIONE
SANCTI ESTIS (1 Peter 1:15)

*Be you also in all manner of
conversation holy*

Spiritual Message

*Very often, saints are thought of as heroes, unconnected with
the hardships and suffering of life. Yet they are people like us,
absorbed in the problems, doubts and expectations that each
one has to face. It is also true, though, that while the saint is one
with his or her humanity, this humanity was lived in the best
of ways. The Gospel is taken as the rule of life, things are looked
at from above. The saint had God as the starting point.
Convinced that there was so much to learn and to love, the
martyr went beyond the limits set by egoism. It is because of this
that the Church professes and believes in the communion of
saints: not only to encourage within the community a
commitment to service among all the baptized, but also to
proclaim to each person that the saints are models of life, fellow
pilgrims who have reached their destination.*

*'The history of the Church is a history of holiness. The New
Testament strongly states this mark of the baptized: they are
"saints" to the extent that, being separate from the world
insofar as the latter is subject to the Evil One, they consecrate
themselves to worshipping the one true God' (IM, 11). The
saints embody hope. For them, what is humanly impossible is
only one side of reality. It needs to be completed by what is
more true and real. It is enough to see their boundless love,
their creativity in the face of difficult situations, their ability to
risk everything for the Word of God. But if the saints still have
something to say to each one of us, it is because they convince
us of the beauty of Christian living, a life committed to
changing history. While visiting the places where they have
lived or which are connected to their memory, let us remember
the words of the Apostle Peter: 'Be you also in all manner of
conversation holy' (1 Peter 1:15).*

THE VATICAN MUSEUMS

RATIAS ET SPECIEM
DESIDERABIT OCULUS (Sirach 40:22)

The eye longs for grace and beauty

Spiritual Introduction

'Art is contemplation. It is the pleasure of a spirit that penetrates nature and discovers that this, too, has a soul. It is the most sublime passion of man, since it is the exercise of thought that tries to understand the universe and to make it understood' (Rodin). In religious art, nature is the life of God itself, that radiates upon the whole of creation and is manifested in its Christ, in whom the whole creation culminates. The source of religious art is the incarnation of Christ. 'I will not cease venerating the human matter through which salvation came to me, because it is a matter full of divine energy and grace' (St John Damascene). Religious art expresses the faith of the Church, the theological vision of the Christian community. It is prayer, a song of praise, a theology in colours, a symphonic expression, a prism of a thousand lights, of the Word who became man and dwelt among us, thus making himself visible and tangible. 'Since he who is the consubstantial image of the Father emptied himself, taking the image of a slave' (Phil 2:6–7), paint and show him who wanted to manifest himself, to everyone's eyes, through words and through colours' (St John Damascene). Religious art is catechesis because it is a radiation of God in Christ. Whether 'it announces through colours and renders present what the Book tells us through words' (Constantinopolitan Council IV, Action X, c. 3), or shows everyone the mysterious face of Christ, Mary or the saints, religious art educates in the faith,

The Last Judgement, **by** Michelangelo, Sistine Chapel, Vatican

because it immerses people in Beauty, which is Truth.

'The eye longs for grace and beauty' (Sir 40:22). For this reason it looks towards the light of the face of Christ and of her who, 'humbler and higher than any creature', gave her consent to the Incarnation. Entering the mystery of God, which has become 'ours' in Christ, is a call to a purification of heart which allows our eyes to see a 'vision' that corresponds to our deepest expectations. A prayer of the Oriental Church recites: 'Christ, let the light of your face shine upon us, so that we may see in it the inaccessible light.' Byzantine liturgy sings: 'Sweet is the light of the sun that shines on our eyes, but sweeter still is the visit of your image, O Christ.'

The Vatican Museums open up an itinerary of beauty and faith and encourage an attitude of prayer. Thus the words of St Paul may be fulfilled: 'All of us, with our unveiled faces like mirrors reflecting the glory of the Lord, are being transformed into the image that we reflect in brighter and brighter glory' (2 Cor 3:18).

Historical and Artistic Summary

PRACTICAL INFORMATION
Vatican City. Entrance on
Viale Vaticano.
C 06 698 33 33.
23, 81, 492 to Piazza del
Risorgimento, or 64 to
St Peter's. Shuttle-bus
between St Peter's and
the Museums.
M Ottaviano.
19 Piazza del
Risorgimento. **Opening
hours** 8.45 a.m.–1.45
p.m. Mon–Fri and last
Sunday of each month;
March–October 8.45
a.m.–4.45 p.m. Mon–Fri,
8.45 a.m.–1.45 p.m. Sat.
Closed on national and
religious holidays. Special
permit necessary for: the
Loggia of Raphael, the
Vatican Library, the
Gallery of Inscriptions
and the Vatican Archives.
Entrance fee. Free on
the last Sunday of each
month. **&** Special tours.
∩ Exhibitions, con-
ferences, films.

***The atrium of Quattro
Cancelli,*** *built by Giuseppe
Camporese in 1792–1793,
was the original entrance to
the Vatican Museums.*

The first museum collection was created in the
Vatican at the behest of Pope Julius II, the
immediate predecessor of Leo X, who owned
the *Belvedere Apollo*, the statue that in the
eighteenth century was to become the model
of ideal classical beauty. But although
Renaissance Popes saw study of antiquity as
the height of culture, they also wanted the
buildings where the life and religious
functions of the Curia took place to be steeped
in the study of theology and biblical interpretation.

The frescoes of the Sistine Chapel, painted by
Michelangelo at two different periods of his
artistic life (1508–1512 and 1536–1541), and for
two different Popes (Julius II and Paul III),
complete the theological programme started
by fifteenth-century painters on the lower
section of the walls. They represent the
universality and the perfect continuity of Old
and New Testament theology. The stories from
Genesis on the vault, framed by the beautiful
Nudes, represent, in the Neoplatonic terms
underpinning Renaissance culture, the course
of human salvation: from the Fall (represented
by the *Drunkenness of Noah*) to our first
Redemption (represented by God's acts of
creation). The focal point of the vault is the
Creation of Man, in which God the Father,
with a touch of his hand, instils life and soul
into Man, still free of sin and depicted in his
perfect human form. But in the vast fresco of
the *Last Judgement* (on the end wall), Michelangelo depicts the drama of a humanity now
aware of sin and of the instruments necessary
for salvation: faith and the Church. It was
completed around the middle of the sixteenth
century, and is imbued with the inner turmoil
of the artist, by then 61 years old. Above all, it
is marked by the dramatic events in the Church

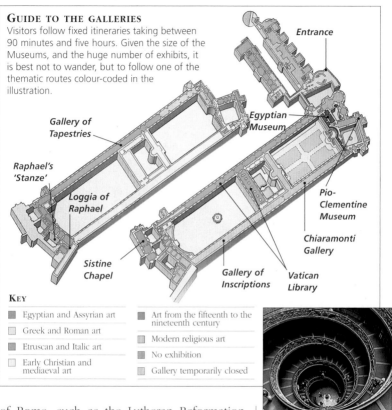

GUIDE TO THE GALLERIES

Visitors follow fixed itineraries taking between 90 minutes and five hours. Given the size of the Museums, and the huge number of exhibits, it is best not to wander, but to follow one of the thematic routes colour-coded in the illustration.

Entrance

Egyptian Museum

Gallery of Tapestries

Raphael's 'Stanze'

Loggia of Raphael

Pio-Clementine Museum

Chiaramonti Gallery

Sistine Chapel

Gallery of Inscriptions

Vatican Library

KEY

- Egyptian and Assyrian art
- Greek and Roman art
- Etruscan and Italic art
- Early Christian and mediaeval art
- Art from the fifteenth to the nineteenth century
- Modern religious art
- No exhibition
- Gallery temporarily closed

of Rome, such as the Lutheran Reformation, and the resulting loss of entire nations like Germany and England, which became Protestant. The naked bodies of saints and devils, of the saved and the damned, stand out against the ultramarine background, giving an overall effect which is strangely archaic, almost medieval in its total lack of any illusion of depth, despite its modern and refined painting technique.

The 'Stanze' bearing his name were painted by Raphael and, after his death, by Giulio Romano and his school under three Popes: Julius II, Leo

The staircase *leading up to the Museums was designed by Giuseppe Momo (1932).*

The Pauline Chapel, commissioned by Paul III from Antonio da Sangallo, was handed over to Michelangelo, who painted his *Conversion of Saul* and *Crucifixion of St Peter* there between 1542 and 1550. It is not open to the public at present.

The Apostolic Vatican Library is part of the museum complex. The library of the Popes is one of the most famous in the world, housing humanity's most important collection of written culture. It was probably founded by Nicholas V on the occasion of the 1450 Jubilee, and was created a public library by Sixtus IV, in 1475. It contains more than **150,000 ancient manuscripts** and countless manuscripts and archives. It has over a **million printed volumes**, including the incunabula (fifteenth-century books) of which the Vatican houses the largest collection. Other treasures of the library are: the Cabinet of Prints, with over **100,000 engravings**, the Vatican Medal Collection, containing a rich collection of **coins and medals**, not all pontifical, and the Christian and Secular Museums, the earliest museums founded in the Vatican.

X and Clement VII. They celebrate the historical continuity of the Church, of which the Popes, appearing in person in the episodes depicted, were the main creators and witnesses. Art and philosophy are the intellectual corollary of theology and the evidence of faith, which make up the Church's earthly history. It is in this spirit, so close to the principles of Church doctrine, that the great works of art preserved in the Vatican Museums come to life.

The general term 'Vatican Museums' covers a multifaceted and diverse reality, forming a complex of stupendous size, with 42,000 square metres open to the public, and over seven kilometres of exhibition space. The oldest parts are the galleries of Greco-Roman sculpture: the Pio-Clementine Museum, founded by Pius VI with lottery money in the late 1700s; the Chiaramonti Gallery (1808) and the 'New Wing' (1816–1822) (both commissioned by Pius VII to compensate for the loss of masterpieces removed to Paris by Napoleon under the Treaty of Tolentino) and the Gregorian Secular Museum, created by Gregory XVI in 1836 at the Lateran Palace, and moved to the Paul VI wing of the Vatican Museums in the 1970s. They hold some of the most famous classical sculptures in the world,

In his **Creation of Man** *(Sistine Chapel, detail, 1508–1512), Michelangelo depicts God who, by touching Adam's hand, imbues him with soul and intelligence.*

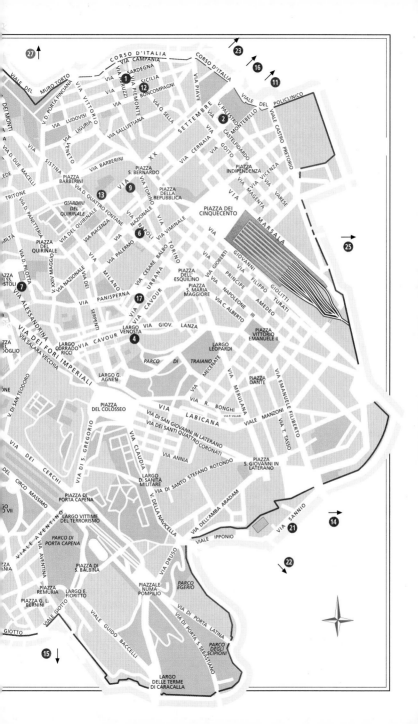

Historical Notes

EASTERN ORTHODOX CHURCHES

1 **Greek Orthodox Church**, 153 Via Sardegna

2 **Russian Orthodox Church**, 69 Via Palestro

3 **Egyptian Coptic Church**, 6 Via San Paolo alla Regola

4 **Ethiopian-Eritrean Community** 5 Via Monte Polacco

The Eastern Orthodox Churches, whether Chalcedonian or not, take their identity from their claim to a special, uninterrupted link with the traditions of the primitive Church.

Their underlying unity is in essence guaranteed by their liturgical tradition, and their acceptance of the doctrine of the Trinity, established at the Councils of Nicaea (325) and Constantinople (381).

The Greek Orthodox community in Rome goes back to the early twentieth century. It had no place of worship of its own until 1955, and depended on the Russian community, which had been established in the mid nineteenth century.

The other communities date from the early 1970s.

ANGLICAN AND AMERICAN EPISCOPALIAN CHURCHES

5 153/b Via del Babuino

6 58 Via Napoli

The Anglican community, which describes itself as 'Catholic and reformed', has been in Rome since 1816. The neo-Gothic church of All Saints (Ogni Santi) is by the famous architect G. E. Street, who also built the American Episcopalian church of St Paul's within the Walls (1875). Although these sister Churches are distinct, they both belong to the worldwide Anglican Communion. The usual form of service is a solemn Eucharist, and they also hold Bible study meetings.

The neo-Gothic church of All Saints

WALDENSIAN (REFORMED) AND METHODIST CHURCH

7 107 Via IV Novembre

8 32 Piazza Cavour

9 Via XX Settembre (corner of Via Firenze)

10 3 Via Banco di Santo Spirito

11 76 Via Batteria Nomentana

The Waldensian Church was founded in 1173 by Peter Waldo as a Church reform movement. At the Synod of Chanforan in 1532, they joined the Reform. The Waldensian Theological College was founded in Piedmont in 1855, and moved to Rome in 1922. It has a presbyterian, synodal structure, based on local, regional and national assemblies. Its doctrine is Calvinist in spirit, based on the Word of God as the only rule of faith and life. Communion recalls Christ, whose presence is understood as real in a spiritual sense. Baptism is performed according to the rite of the early Church. In 1975 the Italian Waldensians and Methodists came together as the Evangelical Waldensian-Methodist Church.

The Methodist Church grew out of the Anglican Church.

LUTHERAN EVANGELICAL CHURCH

⑫ 70 Via Sicilia

The Lutheran Evangelical Church in Italy (CELI) was founded in 1948 on the initiative of Pastor Dahlgrün, in Rome, with six other pastors and lay people. It is represented in Rome by a Dean, elected every five years.

It has a Lutheran, synodal structure, with some variations. The Sunday service is central to the life of the community, with its sermon, prayers and hymns.

Lutherans follow the teaching of Martin Luther, founder of the sixteenth-century Protestant Reformation, and his vision of Holy Scripture as the supreme and sufficient rule of Christian life. The Church is a community in which Scripture is strictly interpreted and the sacraments precisely celebrated, and its central and guiding tenet is the doctrine of justification by faith. Communion is celebrated twice a month, and is a reminder that Christ is spiritually present everywhere.

CHURCH OF SCOTLAND (PRESBYTERIAN)

⑬ 7 Via XX·Settembre

This British Protestant Church embodies the Puritan strain of Calvinist Protestantism. Historically speaking, it represents a kind of second Reform movement. Its organization is collegiate, and based on its Assembly. It promotes ideas of freedom of conscience, and tolerance.

BAPTIST EVANGELICAL CHURCH

⑭ 8 Via delle Spighe
⑮ 21 Via Pullino
⑯ 14 Via Antelao
⑰ 154 Via Urbana
⑱ 27 Via del Teatro Valle
⑲ 124 Via della Lungaretta
⑳ 35 Piazza San Lorenzo in Lucina

Baptists take their inspiration from the sixteenth-century Anabaptists, who proclaimed a radical reform of the Church. The English Baptist mission in Italy began its activities in 1863 and in 1920 the Baptist churches joined together as the Italian Evangelical Baptist Union. Their doctrine is similar to that of other Reformed Churches; they practise adult baptism by immersion, and emphasize the idea of universal priesthood.

Local congregations are autonomous and independent, with a regional, national and international collegiate structure that forms the World Baptist Federation. Its purpose is to promote · fellowship and solidarity among Baptists from different places.

CHURCH OF CHRIST

㉑ 67 Via Sannio
㉒ 63 Via Messala Corvino
㉓ 286 Viale Jonio

This Church was founded in the USA in 1832, and came to the Rome area in 1949.

The Churches of Christ have no ecclesiastical organization, and their local congregations are autonomous. They base their teaching on the Bible, especially the New Testament and its message of Jesus Christ. Believers lead communal prayer, take part in and distribute the Lord's Supper, and can baptize others.

CHURCH OF CHRIST (SEVENTH-DAY ADVENTIST)

㉔ 7 Lungotevere Michelangelo

Founded in America in 1840. Adventists consider Saturday, not Sunday, the Lord's day, and live in expectation of Christ's Second Coming. Italy was the first European country in which they preached, and in 1928, the Italian Union (now Federation) of Adventist Churches was founded. Great importance is given to the Bible, and to a rigid moral life.

SALVATION ARMY

㉕ 42 Via degli Apuli

This is not a church, but an evangelizing movement founded in London in 1865 to proclaim the Gospel to the city's poorest people.

It is organized along quasi-military lines, to ensure its effectiveness. It reached Italy in 1886. It is very open to friendly and co-operative relations with other Christian communities, and turns to the Evangelical Churches for the rituals of baptism and communion.

PLACES OF WORSHIP OF OTHER RELIGIONS

JEWISH COMMUNITY **㉖**

Lungotevere Cenci

The Jewish community that has existed in Rome since the time of the Maccabees (100–60 B.C.) is the oldest of the world's Jewish diaspora. Judaism has strong spiritual links with Christianity, since its identity is based on the divine plan of the God of the Covenant. Jews and Christians thus share a common spiritual heritage, from the Sacred Scripture of the Old Testament to common liturgical features. The synagogue was built in 1904, when the ghetto was abolished, to replace five *scholae* or synagogues. It was designed by two non-Jewish architects in an Art Nouveau style with Middle Eastern elements. Rome's 15,000-strong Jewish community uses it a great deal.

MUSLIM COMMUNITY **㉗**

Centro Islamico Moschea di Roma
1 Via della Moschea

Rome's Islamic community consists of Muslims of many nationalities, all of whom use the large mosque inaugurated in 1995. Islam is the world's second most widespread religion, after Christianity. Its identity centres on the Koran, the sacred book containing the revelation of the Prophet Muhammad. Muslims believe in the virgin birth of Jesus, and in his miracles, but they do not see him as the son of God. Islam is based on five fundamental pillars: the profession of faith – 'There is no God but Allah, and Muhammad is his prophet' (Koran, Sura 4, 136); prayer, carried out at prescribed intervals five times a day; alms-giving; fasting; and pilgrimage.

 N VERITATE ET CARITATE (2 John 3)

In truth and in love

Spiritual Message

*The presence of places of worship belonging to other Churches and ecclesial communities recalls the importance of walking together in 'truth and love' (2 John 3). 'May the ecumenical character of the Jubilee be a concrete sign of the journey which, especially in recent decades, the faithful of the different Churches and ecclesial communities have been making' (IM, 4). The Jubilee is an opportunity to reflect on the significance of belonging to the one Church of Christ, and to live up to its demands for the benefit of humanity. 'Another level is that of the initiatives and collaboration with a humanitarian, social, economic and political aim, which favour a sense of liberty and human advancement' (*Dialogue and Mission, 32).

For this, the knowledge of other religions, in particular of Islam and Judaism, is essential. The person lives this inexhaustible tension towards God which makes life into a constant search. The questions on the meaning of life and the suffering that exists, the aspiration to happiness together with the presence of the mystery which surrounds the person, the beginning and end of history, bear witness to the fact that the world and humanity do not have the last word. It is out of these unanswered questions that Judaism and Christianity believe that God has intervened in history to offer an answer to our questions. Monotheistic religions express a sense of brotherhood. If the Muslim religion witnesses the adoration of the 'one living God, compassionate and all-powerful, creator of heaven and earth, who has talked to mankind' (NA, 3), in the Jewish religion there is present 'the bond that spiritually unites the people of the New Testament with the sons and daughters of Abraham' (NA, 4).

Index of Places

The Continuum Publishing Company
370 Lexington Avenue, New York, NY10017

Original Italian edition
© 1999 Arnoldo Mondadori S.p.A., Milan
Fabio Ratti Editoria S.r.l., Milan

English translation © Geoffrey Chapman

Meditations, Spiritual Introductions, Spiritual Messages translation
© the Vatican
All rights reserved

Library of Congress Cataloging in Publication Data
Pellegrini a Roma per il giubileo dell'anno santo del 2000.
English. *Pilgrims in Rome: The Official Vatican Guide for the Jubilee Year 2000.*
ISBN 0-8264-1187-8
1. Christian pilgrims and pilgrimages – Italy – Rome Guidebooks.
2. Christian shrines – Italy – Rome Guidebooks.
3. Rome (Italy) Guidebooks.
4. Holy Year, 2000.
I. Vatican City. Comitato centrale del grande giubileo dell'anno duemila.
II. Title.
BX2320.5.18P4513 2000
263'.04245632–dc21   99-29745
CIP

PHOTOGRAPHS
Archivio Elemond, Milano
Biblioteca Apostolica Vaticana, Roma
Image Bank, Milano
Musei Vaticani, Roma
Osservatore Romano, Roma
Luciano Pedicini, Napoli

TRANSLATION
Imogen Forster, Irena Hill, with Fiona McKenzie

Companion volume: Pilgrim Prayers

Typeset by Carr Studios

Printed and bound in Spain by Artes Gráficas Toledo, S.A.U.
D.L. TO: 1297- 1999

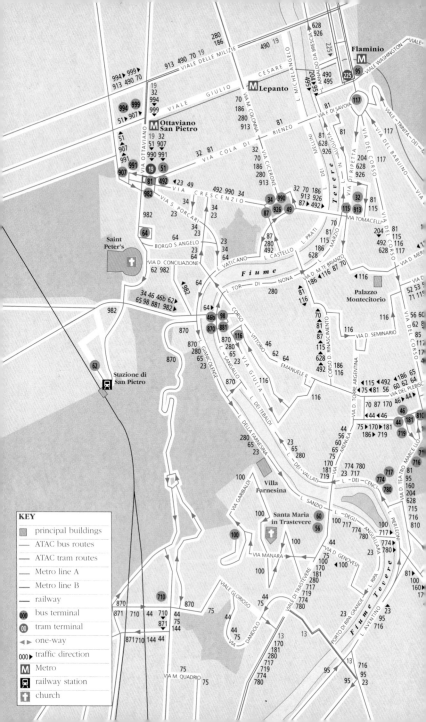